NEW WORLD

Noodles

BILL JONES & STEPHEN WONG

NEW WORLD
Noodles

BILL JONES & STEPHEN WONG

Robert
ROSE

NEW WORLD NOODLES

For complete cataloguing data, see page 6.

DESIGN AND PAGE COMPOSITION:	MATTHEWS COMMUNICATIONS DESIGN
PHOTOGRAPHY:	MARK T. SHAPIRO
ART DIRECTION/FOOD PHOTOGRAPHY:	SHARON MATTHEWS
FOOD STYLIST:	KATE BUSH
PROP STYLIST:	CHARLENE ERRICSON
MANAGING EDITOR:	PETER MATTHEWS
RECIPE EDITOR/TEST KITCHEN:	JUDITH FINLAYSON
INDEXER:	BARBARA SCHON
COLOR SCANS & FILM:	POINTONE GRAPHICS

Cover photo: 5-SPICE CHICKEN WITH GINGER AND SCALLION LO MEIN (PAGE 137)

Distributed in the U.S. by:
Firefly Books (U.S.) Inc.
P.O. Box 1338
Ellicott Station
Buffalo, NY 14205

Distributed in Canada by:
Stoddart Publishing Co. Ltd.
34 Lesmill Road
North York, Ontario
M3B 2T6

ORDER LINES
Tel: (416) 499-8412
Fax: (416) 499-8313

ORDER LINES
Tel: (416) 445-3333
Fax: (416) 445-5967

Published by: Robert Rose Inc. • 156 Duncan Mill Road, Suite 12
Toronto, Ontario, Canada M3B 2N2   Tel: (416) 449-3535

Printed in Canada

1234567 BP 00 99 98 97

CONTENTS

Canadian Cataloguing in Publication Data

Wong, Stephen, 1955–
    New world noodles

Includes index.

ISBN 1-896503-01-2

1. Noodles.   2. Cookery (Pasta).   I. Jones, W.A. (William
Allen), 1959– .   II. Title.

TX809.N65W65 1997   641.8'22   C97-930564-0

ACKNOWLEDGEMENTS

A special thanks to my first cooking teacher, who also happens to be my father, Bill Sr. (a great cook in his own right) and my mother Joan who have always been there to support and love me. This book would not have happened without my wife Lynn, who is a wise critic, has impeccable taste (in men and cats) and never tires of being a guinea pig in my culinary laboratory. (Note: no guinea pigs were harmed in the testing of this book). A big round of applause for Bob, Judith and the team at Robert Rose.

— Bill Jones

My most sincere thanks to all the restaurateurs, chefs, writers, friends and associates in Vancouver who have been like an extended family to me. Their inspiration and support have made my life a joy and this book a reality. In putting this book together, my appreciation goes to Judith Finlayson for her tireless efforts in editing and tasting. Bob Dees for his support and patience, Kate Bush for her lovely food styling, Matthews Communications Design for the superb look of the book and Diane Hargrave for her public relations efforts. Last, but certainly not least, my love and gratitude goes to my wife Nina, my son Christopher and my daughter Brielle for putting up with my noodle obsession.

— Stephen Wong

Photo Prop Credits

The publisher and authors wish to express their appreciation to the following suppliers of props used in the food photography appearing in this book:

URBAN MODE, TORONTO	DISHES, ACCESSORIES, CUTLERY, LINENS
DU VERRE GLASS LIMITED, TORONTO	DISHES, ACCESSORIES, CUTLERY
THE COMPLEAT KITCHEN, TORONTO	DISHES, ACCESSORIES, LINENS

To all my family and friends

— W.A.J.

To Mom and Dad, Sally, Marco and Rebecca
and noodle lovers the world over

— S.W.

$\mathcal{O}$NTRODUCTION

This book is for noodle lovers everywhere. It's for the millions of people across North America who have grown up with pasta and are now expanding their culinary horizons to include the exciting new taste sensations that are unique to noodle cooking.

In Asian countries, of course, noodles aren't exactly new. From Bangkok to Jakarta, from Beijing to Ho Chi Minh City, people have been slurping down noodles — boiled, fried, steamed, scalding hot or refreshingly cool — for centuries. Now the rest of the world is catching on. And a growing number of people are discovering the simplicity, comfort and endless adaptability of noodle dishes.

The relationship between noodles and pasta goes back more than 700 years. It is believed that in the late 13th century, Marco Polo travelled to China and brought noodles back to Italy to add to his country's repertoire of pasta. Today, the cooking styles of East and West meet once again, with noodle dishes that incorporate traditional Asian ingredients and flavors with those of the New World.

As long-time noodle devotees, we've brought to this collection our different perspectives and tastes. The result is a collection of recipes that provides an exciting range of flavor combinations — everything from *Ramen Noodle Soup with Red Snapper, Spinach and Garlic* to *Thick Rice Noodles with Beef, Onion, Corn and Rosemary Sauce* to *Hazelnut Yam Wonton with Maple Syrup*.

Noodles represent a cornucopia of unexplored gastronomic delight. They're quick, easy, nutritious and delicious — an ideal food for today's time-deprived, health-conscious people.

We hope you'll enjoy them as much as we do.

Bill Jones
Stephen Wong

A NOODLE PRIMER

Noodles originated in China and are as diverse and intriguing as their country of origin. Living in a country as disparate as China has made its inhabitants very skilled at modifying basic products to accommodate local tastes. While this provides plenty of interesting variety for consumers, it is also the source of much confusion. In a country that can vary so dramatically from region to region — and with an overwhelming number of noodle manufacturers — product standardization is virtually nonexistent. The result is that noodles, while widely available throughout North America, can vary significantly in quality, nomenclature, size, shape and cooking instructions.

So don't be surprised if you can't find "wunton" noodles at your local Asian market. Sometimes they'll be labelled "wonton" — which can be doubly confusing since these long, very thin noodles are quite different from "wonton wrappers" (which are sheets of noodle dough used to enclose various savory fillings). Similarly, you may not be able to find rice "vermicelli", but only something called "rice stick noodles" — or vice versa — even though they're essentially the same.

As a result, cooking with noodles might take a little extra research, but it's worth the effort. Today, North American consumers can buy virtually any noodle they want in Asian markets and many major supermarkets stock a wide variety of dried or frozen versions. In this book we've included the most common varieties, and a few unusual types are featured for their uniqueness — we hope they'll entice you into the wonderful world of tastes that awaits you in an Asian market.

And if you can't find the noodle specified in the recipe? In just about every case, you can easily substitute another type of noodle or pasta. (See table, page 15, for suggested substitutes.)

Types of Noodles

Noodles fall into three basic categories: those made from wheat, from rice or from other ingredients such as bean starch or buckwheat.

Most wheat noodles are available dried — wonton sheets are an obvious exception. They come in square cakes, bundles of long noodles or as noodle sticks, very much like our familiar dried pastas.

Rice noodles are somewhat more exotic to North Americans. The fresh variety, which are only available in Asian markets, require almost no cooking and have a creamy melt-in-the-mouth consistency that resembles a good custard. Dried rice noodles are widely available as vermicelli, rice stick noodles or as rice paper sheets. They're easily identified by their gray-white translucence, although thin vermicelli is sometimes confused with bean thread noodles. The only noodles we're included from the "other" category are cellophane or bean thread noodles made from bean starch and soba noodles made from buckwheat.

Wheat Noodles (fresh and dried)

Broad wheat noodles. These are thick, flat noodles similar in appearance to fettuccine and available in Asian markets. Fettuccine makes the best pasta substitute.

Chow mein. These are thin, yellow wheat noodles sometimes made with egg. Fresh chow mein is widely available in the refrigerated section of Asian markets and better grocery stores. If your recipe requires a crispy cake of noodles, make sure you buy fresh chow mein — the dried varieties don't stick together very well, although they're fine in other noodle dishes. Most dishes in this book will work with fresh or dried angel hair pasta as a substitute for chow mein. *A word of caution:* Beware of bags of dried deep-fried chow mein which you often see in the Asian section of supermarkets — these may be fine substitutes for croutons in the odd salad, but we've found little use for them otherwise.

Egg noodles. These are the most common type of wheat noodle. Made with whole eggs or yolks, they are richer and softer than plain wheat noodles. If you can't find fresh Asian egg noodles, use dried egg noodles or any long, thin wheat noodle or pasta.

Ramen noodles. These thin, curled Japanese-style noodles are widely available and usually sold as instant meals, with a small seasoning packet. You can discard the seasoning (especially if you're sensitive to MSG since it's always present) and use them in a variety of ways. Some markets also carry bigger packages of ramen noodles, without the flavorings.

NOODLES AT A GLANCE

	NAME	DESCRIPTION	SUBSTITUTE
WHEAT	Broad wheat noodles	Thick, flat; similar to linguine; fresh or dried	Fettuccine
	Chow mein	Thin, yellow; fresh, dried or frozen	Angel hair
	Egg noodles	Wide, flat, yellow; made with eggs fresh or dried	Any long thin noodle/pasta
	Ramen noodles	Thin, curled, Japanese-style; sold dried, in packets	Angel hair or thin noodles
	Shanghai (round) noodles	Thin or thick, round; fresh, cooked or uncooked	Spaghetti (thin) or ziti (thick)
	Thin wheat noodles	Thin, flat, similar to linguine; various lengths; fresh or dried	Linguine or spaghetti
	Udon noodles	Long, thick, round, white; fresh (cooked or uncooked) or frozen	Macaroni or ziti
	Wunton (Wonton) noodles	Very long, thin, round or square very delicate; fresh or dried	Angel hair
	Wonton (Gyoza) wrappers	Round or square sheets; usually in packages of 30-50; fresh	
RICE FRESH	Broad rice noodles	Wide, flat, pure white	Fettuccine
	Round noodles (*Lai Fen*)	Round, white; various sizes	Spaghetti
	Rice noodle sheets	Large, pure white, somewhat gelatinous; often sold in a roll	Lasagna
RICE DRIED	Broad rice stick noodles (Broad vermicelli)	Flat, ribbon-like, greyish white	Fettuccine
	Rice paper sheets	Round or square sheets; very fragile	
	Thin rice stick noodles (Thin vermicelli)	Thin, thread-like, greyish white	Angel hair
OTHER	Soba noodles	Round, thick, gray; made from buckwheat and/or yam/wheat flour; fresh or frozen	Wholewheat linguine
	Bean-based noodles	Transparent, white, very brittle; sometimes called vermicelli; sold in small packages; relatively expensive.	Thin rice stick noodles

Shanghai (Round) noodles. Thick or thin, these noodles are distinguished from many other wheat noodles by their roundness. There are two main versions, a thin noodle similar to spaghetti and a thicker version similar to ziti. (Both types of pasta work as a substitute.) Shanghai noodles cook very quickly and continue to cook in any hot liquid or sauce. Since they can easily become overcooked and glutinous, they should be served quickly. They're widely available, raw or pre-cooked, in Chinese markets and better grocery stores.

Thin wheat noodles. These thin, flat noodles, dried or fresh, are wider than wunton noodles and similar in appearance to linguini. Sometimes made with egg, they come in a variety of sizes and widths. They're available in many ethnic markets but you can easily substitute linguini or spaghetti.

Udon noodles. These long, wide, round white noodles look like space age spaghetti. They're Japanese in origin and are available in fresh, pre-cooked or dried versions.

Wunton (or Wonton) noodles. Not to be confused with wonton wrappers, these are very long, thin noodles, round or square, sometimes made with egg and usually only available in Asian markets. They are very fine and delicate should be cooked very briefly to reach their peak of perfection. The dried versions are often flavored with ingredients such as shrimp, egg, carrot and spinach. Fresh or dried angel hair pasta can easily be substituted.

Wonton (Gyoza) wrappers. These are square or round sheets of fresh noodle dough usually sold in packs of 30 to 50 sheets and found in the cooler or freezer section of Asian markets and better grocery stores. They can be filled with a wide variety of sweet or savory fillings. One word of caution: They become brittle when they dry out so opened packages should be covered with a damp towel.

RICE NOODLES (FRESH)

Broad rice noodles. Broad, flat and pure white these are simply rice noodle sheets cut into strips. They're wonderful with sauces and require very little cooking. Usually, running hot water over the noodles before adding to a hot sauce is adequate.

Round noodles (*Lai Fen*). These round, white noodles come in a variety of sizes and are often sold pre-cooked in vacuum packages. Spaghetti makes a good substitute, although the unique texture and taste of the Lai Fen will be lost. They're also available in a dried version.

Rice noodle sheets. These large, pure white sheets of gelatinous noodle dough are often sold rolled. When served, they're usually stuffed with various fillings. The noodles dry out over time and become brittle and hard to work with. If they're hard to unroll, a quick dip in hot water will soften them and make them easier to use. Noodle sheets are only available fresh and almost exclusively in Chinese markets.

RICE NOODLES (DRIED)

Broad rice stick noodles (Broad vermicelli). These flat, ribbon-like grayish-white noodles, similar to fettuccine, are simply a broader version of thin rice stick noodles (see following), distinguished by the fact that they require a longer soaking or cooking time. They, too, are quite widely available.

Thin rice stick noodles (Thin vermicelli). These bundles of wispy noodles look like translucent angel hair pasta and they're available in Asian markets and better grocery stores. The term "rice stick" may be misleading as it applies to a wide range of noodle widths and shapes. Vermicelli usually refers to this fine noodle although we have seen broad rice stick noodles classified as vermicelli. There are also varieties of thin flat rice noodles from Vietnam or Thailand, similar to linguini, which are widely available and often labelled as "rice stick noodles."

Rice paper sheets. These very fragile sheets of dried rice noodle are made from a mixture of rice flour, water and salt which is rolled thin and dried on bamboo mats. They come in rounds or squares and must be dipped in hot water to make them pliable. They usually come from Vietnam or Thailand, and are always available in Asian markets.

OTHER TYPES OF NOODLES

Soba noodles. These gray-colored noodles are a Japanese invention, made from buckwheat, often with wheat or yam flour added. They come in a wide variety of textures, shapes and sizes and the Japanese love them as an ice-cold salad with a soy-based dip. They're available in a wide variety of health food, Japanese and Asian markets. Buckwheat soba, which is wheat-free, is often used in gluten-free diets. Soba noodles are mealy, like whole wheat pasta and they become very mushy if overcooked.

Bean-based noodles (Bean thread, Cellophane, Glass thread, etc.) Transparent, white and extremely brittle, there rather exotic noodles are available in a variety of styles. Their chewy texture readily absorbs sauces and flavorings, which makes them particularly appropriate for braised dishes involving meats and seafood. Glass thread or bean thread noodles, also called vermicelli on occasion, are the most common version. They are often sold in small packages, not only because they're relatively expensive, but also because they are very difficult to separate when dry.

Cooking Noodles

Whether fresh or dried, the most important thing to remember about noodles is that they cook quickly and turn starchy when overcooked. So watch them carefully! You should also know that fresh noodles are quite perishable. The sooner you eat them, the better they are — 1 or 2 days after purchase is ideal but they'll usually last about a week in your refrigerator and up to 2 months in your freezer. Dried noodles will last almost indefinitely if kept dry in an airtight package.

We usually prefer fresh noodles to their dried counterparts, although some noodles such as bean thread noodles or rice paper sheets are only sold in the dried form. Since noodles dishes are usually cooked very quickly, all the ingredients should be prepared in advance. The noodles themselves can be cooked in boiling, salted water or simply soaked in boiling water for a specified period of time. As a rule, noodles have more starch than pasta, so it's important they're not overcooked or over-soaked. If that happens, you'll end up with a glutinous mass.

When cooking or soaking noodles, you should stir to separate the strands a minute or two after they're immersed in water. Once they're ready, they're drained and usually tossed with a little oil until they're needed. Although the oil helps to keep them from sticking together, if they're left too long (10 minutes maximum), the noodles will form a clump. Spreading them out on a plate or tray, rather than lumping them in a bowl will help.

Another problem with the lack of standardization is that often basic product information varies dramatically — one package will suggest cooking a specific noodle for 5 minutes, another will say it requires 10. Initially, use the noodles we've recommended and follow our instructions. Soon you'll achieve a comfort level with noodles and be able to figure things out for yourself.

Some varieties of noodles contain ingredients that cause them to emit a pungent aroma. If this is a problem, it can be corrected by tossing them with some Chinese red, or balsamic vinegar and a little sesame oil. (Toss 1 lb (500 g) noodles with 1 tbsp (15 mL) of vinegar and 2 tsp (10 mL) of sesame oil.)

And finally, a word on quantities: we've allowed 1/4 lb (125 g) of fresh noodles per person and 2 oz (50 g) dried. This makes a substantial main course.

*T*HE NOODLE PANTRY

In this book, we've focused primarily on ingredients that are easily accessible. Most are available in your neighborhood supermarket or specialty food store. Our sauces will usually work with a wide variety of noodle types and pastas. To achieve great results, you don't need to follow the recipe exactly. Let your fridge, pocketbook and the availability of ingredients be your guide to great-tasting meals.

USING HERBS AND SPICES

Herbs are always better fresh. Dried herbs usually have less flavor and aromatic oils. However, they're usually more intense (often bitterly so) and should be used in a ratio of 1 tbsp (15 mL) fresh to 1 tsp (5 mL) dried. Rosemary is an exception — the dried version has slightly less flavor than the fresh, but it's used in roughly equal amounts.

Spices should be purchased in small quantities and stored in a dark, dry place since they tend to lose their flavor over time. For best results, prepare whole spices as needed — we use an electric coffee grinder. Gently heating dry spices in an oven, or dry sauté pan over medium heat, usually improves their flavor.

TOOLS AND TECHNIQUES

All the recipes in this book benefit from the advance preparation of ingredients. Because we are often cooking the ingredients very quickly, it's important that the vegetables are cut in ways that make use of their individual characteristics.

To make your work easier, we recommend you purchase a good stainless steel chef's knife — it's a lifetime investment. But inexpensive Chinese or Japanese vegetable cleavers also work very well. If possible, make sure you buy a stainless steel version.

Sometimes, we call for "shredded" fish or meat in a recipe. This involves cutting the fish or meat into thin slices and cutting each slice into 1/4-inch (5 mm) pieces.

FLAVORFUL FUNDAMENTALS

BLACK BEAN SAUCE

This fermented and salted soy bean product is widely available in small glass jars, often with the addition of other seasonings such as garlic.

CHAR SUI SAUCE

This is the sweet, spiced paste that seasons Chinese barbecued pork. It's especially good when balanced with a little rice vinegar to create a sweet-and-sour effect.

CHILI (HOT PEPPER) SAUCE

There are many varieties of chili or hot sauce, each with subtle flavor differences. Many provide excellent flavor, including the old standby, Tabasco sauce. When we suggest that you "pass the hot sauce," this is what we mean.

CHILI PASTE

Asian markets and better grocery store carry a wide variety of chili pastes. Some are mixed with garlic, ginger and other spices. Check the label for ingredients. Start with a simple version, then experiment.

CHILIES

Here's the ultimate "fusion" ingredient. Chilies been exported and integrated into cuisines around the world. As a general rule, the smaller the pepper, the hotter it is. The seeds are hard to digest and the inner membrane supplies most of the heat, so remove them with a knife if you want to lessen the impact. Wear rubber gloves if you're sensitive — and don't touch your eyes!

CHINESE BROCCOLI (GAI LAN)

This bright olive-green vegetable is highly nutritious and loaded with iron, calcium and vitamins A and C. The flavor is earthy and slightly bitter. It's traditionally served blanched, with a drizzle of oyster sauce on top. Substitute broccoli, rapini or kale.

CHINESE CHIVES

Asian markets sell a wide variety of chives, which come in yellow, flowering, garlic and green varieties. Choose chives that are firm and not wilted. Their pungent flavor adds a distinctive taste to most dishes in this book. If you can't find the Chinese version, regular chives or even green onion tops will do.

CHINESE GREEN CABBAGE (SUI CHOY)

North Americans often call this soft green vegetable "Napa cabbage." The mildly flavored leaves, which cook very quickly and reach their peak of flavor when barely wilted, are excellent in soups or lightly stir-fried in noodles dishes. For the best results, add the cabbage at the end of cooking and barely warm through. A good substitute is finely sliced green cabbage.

CHINESE MUSTARD (GAI CHOY)

These greens are often called Chinese mustard cabbage and are used in stir-frys and soups. They're often preserved in a wide variety of forms (pickled, salted, fermented, etc.). Choose mustards that have firm, juicy stems and whole, unwilted leaves. Substitute arugula, spinach, or rapini.

CHINESE WHITE CABBAGE (BOK CHOY)

A couple of dozen variants of Chinese white cabbage are sporadically available in our markets. Bok choy, which is sold as a mature vegetable or in a young "baby" version, is one of the most common. Crunchy in texture and slightly bitter in taste, it has a thick white stem bordered by rich green leaves. Substitute Napa cabbage or savoy cabbage.

CILANTRO

This herb looks like Italian parsley but it's distinguished by its wonderfully robust smell. We use it often in sauces and frequently as a final garnish. Also sold as fresh coriander leaves.

CURRY

In India, every region and village has its own variation of curry. It is actually a blend of spices, such as turmeric, cardamom, cinnamon and tamarind. Most commercial varieties are available in different strengths, ranging from mild to hot. Dry curry powder should be heated (preferably with oil) to release the flavors. Madras curry powder, which is available in Asian markets, is sweeter and less bitter than most commercial versions and we recommend its use. Curry paste, available in jars or tins, works best in dishes where the curry isn't thoroughly cooked in oil.

FISH SAUCE

Originally from Southeast Asia — where it's an indispensable part of Vietnamese and Thai cookery — fish sauce lends a rich and exotic flavor to many dishes. It's made from salted, fermented fish, but the fishy aroma dissipates when it's cooked.

5-SPICE POWDER

This is a blend of seasonings (like curry) and comes in several variations. It's usually a mix of star anise, fennel seed, cinnamon, Szechuan peppercorns and cloves.

GARLIC

The king of seasonings, garlic is widely used in cultures all over the globe. Our recipes can easily handle additional quantities of garlic — if you're a fan of this pungent bulb, don't be afraid to add as much as you like. Garlic tempers its astringency when cooked.

GINGER ROOT

Only fresh ginger root — not the dried powder — should be used in Asian-style cooking. It keeps well in the fridge for 2 weeks and can easily be shredded, diced or sliced. It's widely available — and good for you; recent studies suggest that it has the effect of purifying the blood and lowering cholesterol.

HOISIN SAUCE

Hoisin is another fermented soybean product made from a combination of soy, garlic, vinegar, sugar and spices. Commercial versions often contain other ingredients, such as sweet potato or yam purée. Sweet and spicy, it is great with meat — especially pork and duck.

JAPANESE 7-SPICE *(SCHICHIMI)*

This delicious blend of red pepper, dried mandarin orange peel, *nori* seaweed, sesame seeds and other ingredients makes a wonderful addition to some noodle dishes. If you can't find it, use cracked black pepper, or lemon pepper, instead.

LEMON GRASS

A long woody grass which lends a citrus-like flavor to Southeast Asian cooking, lemon grass is available in Asian markets and some supermarkets. In recipes it's "smashed", which means it's broken up with the flat side of a knife or cleaver, then sliced into 1-inch (2.5 cm) pieces to release its aromatic oils. It's a little difficult to locate; if you can't find it, lemon zest makes an acceptable substitute.

MUSHROOMS

Three main types of Chinese mushrooms are commonly available in Asian markets.

Dried black mushrooms, often called by their Japanese name, *shiitake*, add texture and a robust flavor to dishes. The large ones, with a white cracked design on top, are the most highly valued — and expensive.

Wood ear fungus is a dry, brittle mushroom which is soaked and finely shredded before use.

Straw mushrooms are a small, plump variety, usually sold only in cans. Rinsed and sautéed, they add an interesting texture and flavor to any dish.

OILS

We feel that vegetable oil is the best all-round choice for stir-frying and deep-frying. Olive oil, which we use in a couple of Italian-influenced recipes, comes in many forms. Extra virgin oil is used mainly for flavoring, not cooking. Regular olive oil is lighter in color and taste and is fine for roasting and sautéeing at moderate temperatures. Toasted sesame oil is a rich dark oil used primarily for flavoring.

OYSTER SAUCE

This ancient brew is made from boiling large vats of oysters, soya sauce, salt, spices and seasonings. Commercial preparations vary widely in salt and MSG content, and some contain cornstarch as a thickener. It can be used from the bottle as a dip or to add flavor to vegetables.

PEPPER

Whole peppercorns are very flavorful and should be ground as needed in a peppermill. White pepper is stronger and hotter than black pepper, so less is required.

PLUM SAUCE

This is a sweet, tart, spiced purée of plums, ginger, chili, vinegar, sugar and spices. Plum sauce varies widely in its consistency, sweetness, and level of spice. It's a great addition to sauces and makes a wonderful glaze for roasted poultry, meats, seafood or vegetables.

SALT

Although ordinary table salt is fine, sea salt has a sweeter, less metallic taste and we recommend its use in all our recipes. The coarse salt can be freshly ground in a grinder or crushed with a mortar and pestle.

SESAME SEEDS

Sesame seeds have a delicious, nutty flavor and we often suggest the toasted version as a finish to a dish. To toast sesame seeds, simply heat a dry sauté pan, add the seeds and stir until they begin to change color. Remove from heat immediately, as they will continue cooking. The seeds should be nicely golden.

SOYA SAUCE

Soya sauce, which has been around for 3,000 years, is the product of fermented soybeans. Experiment to find a brand that suits your taste. It keeps indefinitely, even when stored at room temperature. People with a gluten allergy should read soya sauce labels carefully, as some brands contain flour.

Light soya, which is the least aged, is the one most often used in cooking. Several great Japanese and Chinese products are on the market, including low-sodium and wheat-free versions. Dark soya is slightly thicker from added caramel and aged longer. It's the preferred soya for dips, braising and seasoning noodle dishes. Sweet soya (*ketchup manis*), which is almost syrupy in texture, is made by adding palm syrup and herbs and spices after fermentation; it's available in medium and sweet versions. If you can't locate a bottle, make our substitute (see recipe, page 36).

SPICY BEAN PASTE

This spicy paste has many versions, but basically they're all composed of chilies, spices and a fermented soybean paste. They vary widely in flavor and degree of spicing. Some varieties are extremely pungent and should be used with great restraint.

STAR ANISE

This is the seed pod of a tropical tree. It has an intense licorice taste, so use with caution — it can be overpowering.

STARCHES

We've used cornstarch to thicken cooking liquids to make many of the sauces in this book. For noodles, a thick sauce is desirable since it sticks to the noodles and coats the mouth. Heat will cause the starch molecules to expand and bind, so the starch should always be mixed into a paste with cold water before adding it to the hot liquid. The sauce will continue to thicken as it heats; if it's too thin for your taste, add a little more starch. Thin with stock or water if you happen to add too much.

SZECHUAN PEPPERCORNS

These are actually not peppercorns (which are seeds), but dried reddish-brown berries first discovered in the Szechuan region of China. They have a spicy, complex, slightly numbing flavor, and are among the most ancient seasonings used in Chinese cooking. For best results, toast them before use in a dry skillet.

TOFU (BEANCURD)

Beancurd is made from soybeans that have been ground and heated to solidify the soy proteins. It has been nourishing Asians for nearly a millennium. It's rich in protein, nutritious and inexpensive. It comes in many forms — from soft and silky to firm and dense. Always buy tofu as fresh as possible and use within a few days of opening the package.

VINEGAR

Rice vinegar is less acidic than its western counterparts, and it's an important component of Asian cooking. White rice vinegar is smooth and mild and is used to balance hot and sweet flavorings. Darker vinegars come in black, red and dark-brown versions. They are made from the fermentation of rice or different grains such as wheat, millet and sorghum. Balsamic vinegar, which is made from wood-aged, fermented wine vinegar, can be substituted for the darker vinegars.

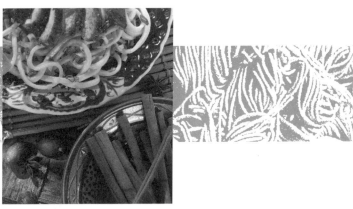

$\mathcal{B}$ASICS

HOME-STYLE 5-SPICE MIX

This mixture is our interpretation of the classic Chinese seasoning, 5-Spice Powder. The commercial version can be found in Asian markets.

2 tbsp	fennel seeds	25 mL
2 tbsp	clove sticks	25 mL
2 tbsp	star anise	25 mL
2 tbsp	Szechuan peppercorns	25 mL
2	cinnamon sticks (or 2 tsp [10 mL] ground cinnamon)	2

1. In a nonstick pan over medium-high heat, cook the spices, shaking the pan constantly. When the pan just begins to smoke, remove from the heat. Transfer contents to a plate to cool.

2. In a small coffee or spice grinder (you can also use a mortar and pestle, blender or food processor) grind spices until a fine powder is obtained. Transfer to a small, sealable plastic container and reserve until needed.

AROMATIC CHICKEN STOCK

**MAKES ABOUT
18 CUPS (4.5 L)**

*Basic chicken stock is
probably the best liquid
to add to any sauce —
whether meat-, fish- or
vegetable-based.*

*Chicken necks and backs
are usually available at
the meat counter of
grocery stores.*

*The stock will keep
refrigerated for about
1 week or it can be
frozen and kept for up
to 2 months.*

5 lb	chicken backs and necks, rinsed to remove any blood	2 kg
3	large onions, peeled and roughly chopped	3
3	carrots, peeled and roughly chopped	3
3	celery stalks, roughly chopped	3
1/2	garlic head	1/2
1	piece ginger root, about 2 inches (5 cm) long	1
1	small handful mixed herbs (cilantro, basil, etc.)	1
5	whole black peppercorns	5
1 tbsp	salt (preferably sea salt)	15 mL
20 cups	water	5 L

1. Place ingredients in a large stockpot, adding more water, if necessary, to cover. Bring mixture to a boil; reduce heat and simmer gently for 3 hours, skimming occasionally to remove any foam or impurities that rise to the top. Try not to let the mixture boil or the broth will be cloudy.

2. Strain into a container and cool to room temperature before refrigerating. (If hot stock is placed directly in the fridge, it will sometimes sour.) For a more intensely flavored stock, let liquid cool and remove any fat from the top; return stock to pot and, over low heat, simmer until volume is reduced by half.

RICH BEEF STOCK

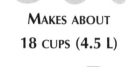

**MAKES ABOUT
18 CUPS (4.5 L)**

*Slowly roasting the beef
bones caramelizes their
sugars and enriches this
stock. Try not to burn
the bones, or the stock
will be bitter.*

*The stock will keep
refrigerated for about
1 week or it can be
frozen and kept for up
to 2 months.*

**Preheat oven to 400° F (200° C)
Large roasting pan**

5 lb	beef bones (shin or neck), rinsed to remove any blood	2 kg
3	large onions, peeled and roughly chopped	3
3	carrots, peeled and roughly chopped	3
3	celery stalks, roughly chopped	3
1	head garlic	1
1/2 cup	tomato paste	125 mL
3	bay leaves	3
1	small handful thyme	1
1	small handful rosemary	1
1	small handful marjoram	1
1	bunch parsley stalks	1
5	whole black peppercorns	5
20 cups	water	5 L

1. Place bones in pan and roast until lightly golden, about 2 hours. Add vegetables and garlic and roast 1 hour. Add tomato paste, stirring to coat. Roast 30 minutes.

2. Place roasted bones and vegetables in a large stock pot; add remaining ingredients. Add more water, if necessary, to cover. Bring mixture to a boil; reduce heat and simmer 6 to 8 hours, skimming occasionally to remove any foam or impurities that rise to the top. Try not to let the mixture boil or the broth will be cloudy.

3. Strain into a container and cool to room temperature before refrigerating. (If hot stock is placed directly in the fridge, it will sometimes sour.) For a more intensely flavored stock, let liquid cool and remove any fat from the top; return stock to pot and, over low heat, simmer until volume is reduced by half.

AROMATIC FISH STOCK

MAKES ABOUT
18 CUPS (4.5 L)

A good fish stock is clear and has a pleasant fish flavor. Acidity, in the form of wine or lemon juice, helps to make the stock clear.

Halibut, sole or other white-fleshed fish make the best stock.

Canned or bottled clam juice makes a good substitute for fish stock but be sure to tell your guests it's part of the recipe since it can trigger a reaction for people with shellfish allergies.

The stock will keep refrigerated for about 1 week or it can be frozen and kept for up to 2 months.

5 lb	fish bones, rinsed under cold water to remove any blood	2.5 kg
3	large onions, peeled and roughly chopped	3
2	leeks, washed and roughly chopped	2
3	celery stalks, roughly chopped	3
1	head fennel, diced	1
3	bay leaves	3
1	small handful mixed herbs (cilantro, basil, etc.)	1
5	whole black peppercorns	5
2 tsp	fennel seed	10 mL
2 tsp	allspice	10 mL
2 tsp	cilantro	10 mL
2 cups	white wine	500 mL
20 cups	water	5 L

1. Place ingredients in a large stockpot, adding more water, if necessary, to cover. Bring mixture to a boil; reduce heat and simmer gently for 3 hours, skimming occasionally to remove any foam or impurities that rise to the top. Try not to let the mixture boil or the broth will be cloudy.

2. Strain into a container and cool to room temperature before refrigerating. (If hot stock is placed directly in the fridge, it will sometimes sour.) For a more intensely flavored stock, let liquid cool and remove any fat from the top; return stock to pot and, over low heat, simmer until volume is reduced by half.

AROMATIC VEGETABLE STOCK

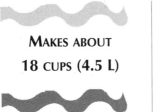

**MAKES ABOUT
18 CUPS (4.5 L)**

*A good vegetable stock
will add life to any soup
or sauce. You can add
other vegetables, such as
parsnips, cabbages, fen-
nel, kale, and cauli-
flower. Roasting the veg-
etables first makes a nice
brown stock which can
be further enhanced by
adding 1 tbsp (15 mL)
tomato paste.*

*The stock will keep
refrigerated for about
1 week or it can be
frozen and kept for up
to 2 months.*

3	large onions, peeled and roughly chopped	3
2	leeks, washed and roughly chopped	2
5	celery stalks, roughly chopped	5
3	bay leaves	3
1	small handful mixed herbs (cilantro, basil, etc.)	1
5	whole black peppercorns	5
1/2	head garlic	1/2
1	slice ginger root	1
1 tsp	fennel seed	5 mL
1 tsp	allspice	5 mL
1 tsp	cilantro leaves	5 mL
2 cups	white wine	500 mL
20 cups	water	5 L

1. Place ingredients in a large stockpot, adding more water, if necessary, to cover. Bring mixture to a boil; reduce heat and simmer gently for 3 hours, skimming occasionally to remove any foam or impurities that rise to the top. Try not to let the mixture boil or the broth will be cloudy.

2. Strain into a container and cool to room temperature before refrigerating. (If hot stock is placed directly in the fridge, it will sometimes sour.) For a more intensely flavored stock, let liquid cool; return stock to pot and, over low heat, simmer until volume is reduced by half.

UPPER: STEAMED BEEF AND CILANTRO BUNDLES (PAGE 46) ➤
LOWER: SMOKED SALMON AND CREAM CHEESE ON A CRISPY NOODLE PANCAKE (PAGE 38)

NUOC CHAM

MAKES ABOUT 2 CUPS

(500 mL)

This all-purpose dipping sauce can be found in most Vietnamese kitchens. It makes a wonderful dressing for noodles and vegetables.

The sauce can be kept covered and refrigerated for up to 3 days.

1/3 cup	sugar (or to taste)	75 mL
1 cup	warm water	250 mL
1 or 2	small red chilies, seeded and minced (or 2 tsp [10 mL] dried chili flakes)	1 or 2
2 tbsp	white rice vinegar	25 mL
2 tbsp	fresh lime juice	25 mL
1 tbsp	minced garlic	15 mL
1/2 cup	fish sauce	125 mL
1	small carrot, peeled and finely shredded	1

1. In a small bowl, combine sugar and warm water, stirring until sugar is dissolved. Add remaining ingredients, except carrots, and mix well. Allow to stand for at least 30 minutes to develop flavors.

2. Just before serving the sauce, wrap shredded carrots in a clean towel and squeeze to remove excess moisture; add carrots to sauce.

< CURRY-FRIED TOFU SOUP WITH VEGETABLES AND UDON NOODLES (PAGE 52)

SPICY SESAME VINAIGRETTE

**MAKES ABOUT
1 1/2 CUPS (375 mL)**

This is a classic dipping sauce for Chinese dumplings but it also works well with steamed prawns, crab or even fresh oysters.

The sauce will keep, covered and refrigerated, for up to 3 days.

1/2 cup	soya sauce	125 mL
1/2 cup	Chinese red vinegar *or* balsamic vinegar	125 mL
1 tbsp	chili oil *or* 1-2 jalapeno peppers, thinly sliced	15 mL
1 tbsp	sesame oil	15 mL
1 tbsp	minced ginger root	15 mL
2 tbsp	water *or* chicken stock	25 mL

1. In a small bowl, combine all ingredients. Set aside for 30 minutes to develop flavors. Serve at room temperature as a dipping sauce or a dressing for seafood.

GINGER SUNOMONO DRESSING

**MAKES ABOUT
1 CUP (250 mL)**

This light, all-purpose dressing hails from Japan. It's great for dressing salads or to subtly enhance the flavor of poached or steamed seafood.

The next time you're stumped for a green salad dressing, try adding 2 tsp (10 mL) mandarin orange zest and 1 tbsp (15 mL) concentrated orange juice to this recipe.

The dressing will keep in the refrigerator for up to 3 days.

1 tbsp	sugar or *mirin*	15 mL
1/3 cup	rice vinegar	75 mL
1 1/2 tbsp	soya sauce	20 mL
1/2 cup	AROMATIC FISH STOCK (see recipe, page 31) *or* AROMATIC CHICKEN STOCK (see recipe, page 29)	125 mL
2 tbsp	finely grated ginger root	25 mL

1. In a small nonreactive (or nonstick) saucepan, combine sugar and vinegar. Stir over medium heat until sugar is dissolved.

2. Remove from heat, add remaining ingredients and mix well. Allow to cool before serving.

SWEET SOYA SAUCE SUBSTITUTE

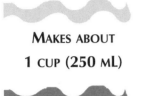

**MAKES ABOUT
1 CUP (250 mL)**

*This sauce will keep in
the refrigerator for up to
2 weeks.*

1 cup	dark soya sauce	250 mL
2 tbsp	brown sugar	25 mL
1 tbsp	dark molasses	15 mL

1. Place ingredients in a small bowl; mix well to combine. Cover and store in refrigerator until needed.

APPETIZERS

SMOKED SALMON AND CREAM CHEESE ON A CRISPY NOODLE PANCAKE

SERVES 4

AS AN APPETIZER

The silken texture of the salmon and the crunchy noodle cake makes a great combination.

The components can be made well in advance. Keep the pancakes in a warm oven and assemble just before serving.

Preheat oven to 250° F (120° C)

4 oz	smoked salmon, or 5-SPICE MAPLE CURED SALMON (see recipe, page 92)	125 g
1 cup	cream cheese, softened	250 mL
2 tbsp	chopped chives	25 mL
4 cups	fresh chow mein noodles	1L
1 tsp	sesame oil	5 mL
1	green onion, thinly sliced	1
1 tbsp	vegetable oil	15 mL
	Salt and pepper to taste	

1. On a cutting board, stretch out 12 inches (30 cm) of plastic wrap. Lay paper-thin slices of salmon on the plastic, their edges overlapping slightly. Spread cream cheese evenly over salmon layer. Sprinkle with chopped chives. Using the plastic wrap to help you, tightly roll the salmon mixture into a log. Cut into thin slices and set aside.

2. In a heatproof bowl or pot, cover noodles with boiling water and let soak for 5 minutes. Drain and toss with sesame oil and green onions.

3. In a nonstick wok or skillet, heat oil for 30 seconds. Add half the noodles, press down with a spatula to flatten and cook on one side until golden, about 5 minutes. Flip, press down hard and cook the other side for an additional 5 minutes. Season with salt and pepper and drain on a paper towel. Keep warm in oven. Repeat procedure with remaining noodles.

4. Cut the pancakes into eighths, top each with two salmon rolls and garnish with green onion or chives.

Tortillas Stuffed with Rice Noodles, Shredded Pork and a Spicy Bean Dressing

SERVES 4

AS AN APPETIZER

These delicious tortillas make a great appetizer, as well as a fast and nutritious lunch.

To freshen tortillas, heat them in a dry skillet, one at a time, for 1 or 2 minutes or heat in microwave for 30 seconds.

You can buy freshly cooked barbecue pork in Chinatown; otherwise, try substituting leftover roast beef, pork or chicken.

Dressing:

1 tbsp	chili bean paste	15 mL
2 tbsp	chunky peanut butter, at room temperature	25 mL
1 tsp	minced ginger root	5 mL
1 tbsp	rice vinegar	15 mL
1 tbsp	mayonnaise	15 mL

Rolls:

2 oz	thin vermicelli (thin rice stick noodles) *or* angel hair pasta	50 g
	Vegetable oil for coating noodles	
4	large flour tortillas	4
1 cup	bean or alfalfa sprouts	250 mL
1 cup	shredded barbecue pork *or* roast pork, beef or chicken	250 mL

1. In a small bowl, combine chili bean paste, peanut butter, ginger root, vinegar and mayonnaise; mix well. If dressing appears too thick, dilute with hot water until a pouring consistency is obtained.

2. In a heatproof bowl or pot, cover noodles with boiling water and let stand for 3 minutes. (If using pasta, prepare according to package directions.) Drain, coat with a little oil, and set aside.

3. Lay a tortilla on work surface. Place one quarter of the noodles on the middle of the tortilla, drizzle one quarter of the dressing over the noodles, then add one quarter of the sprouts and barbecue pork. Lift one side of the tortilla over to cover the filling, fold both ends up so the contents are contained and roll into a tight cylinder. Secure with a toothpick. Repeat procedure with remaining ingredients.

SALMON SPRING ROLLS WITH ORANGE DIPPING SAUCE

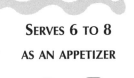

SERVES 6 TO 8

AS AN APPETIZER

Orange and salmon make a delightful variation on the traditional spring roll. The rolls should be cooked as soon as they're assembled, otherwise the dough gets soggy. But you can cook them ahead and reheat in a 350° F (180° C) oven for 3 minutes just before serving

For a quick main dish, try frying the marinated salmon in butter with a touch of minced ginger root. When it's cooked, splash with 2 to 3 tbsp (25 to 45 mL) fresh orange juice and serve with steamed rice noodles and a green salad.

Dipping Sauce:

1/2 cup	orange marmalade	125 mL
1/2 cup	cider vinegar	125 mL
2	small red chilies, seeded and finely chopped	2
1/4 tsp	salt	1 mL

Marinade for Fish:

1 tbsp	minced ginger root	15 mL
2 tbsp	dry sherry or white wine	25 mL
1/2 tsp	salt	2 mL
Pinch	sugar	Pinch
1 tbsp	soya sauce	15 mL
2 tsp	sesame oil	10 mL
2 tsp	cornstarch	10 mL

Spring Rolls:

1 lb	boneless salmon fillet, cut into finger-sized sticks	500 g
2 cups	bean sprouts	500 mL
2 cups	garlic chives, or Chinese flowering chives, cut into 2-inch (5 cm) sticks *or* leeks, blanched and sliced into thin strips	500 mL
1	can (6 oz [150 g]) sliced bamboo shoots, drained (optional)	1
20 sheets	egg roll wrappers	20 sheets
1	egg, beaten	1
1-2 cups	vegetable oil	250-500 mL
4	sprigs cilantro (optional)	4

1. In a small saucepan, combine ingredients for dipping sauce. Bring to a boil, stirring, until marmalade dissolves. Remove from heat and allow to cool.

2. In a medium-sized bowl, whisk together ingredients for marinade. Add salmon, mix well and let marinate for 10 minutes.

3. In a bowl combine bean sprouts, chives and bamboo shoots. Mix well and set aside.

4. Lay one wrapper on a work surface so it looks like a diamond-shaped square. Put one piece of salmon and 1 heaping tbsp (15-20 mL) of vegetable mixture in the center. Fold the edge of the wrapper closest to you over the filling, do the same with the sides, then roll into a tight cylinder. Brush the remaining edge of the wrapper with beaten egg, seal and set aside. Repeat until all the wrappers are filled.

5. Heat oil in a small skillet over medium-high heat until a strip of wonton wrapper dropped in the oil sizzles and floats to the top immediately. Add rolls in small batches and fry until golden brown, about 2 minutes per side. Drain on paper towel and keep warm.

6. Transfer spring rolls to a platter. Garnish with cilantro and orange slices, if desired, and serve with dipping sauce on the side.

CHOPPED CHICKEN IN LETTUCE WRAP WITH CRISPY GLASS NOODLES

SERVES 4 TO 6 AS AN APPETIZER

A great way to start a dinner party — especially on the 7th day of the Chinese New Year, when it's everyone's birthday. The deep-fried bean thread noodles are light and crispy and add visual drama as a garnish, especially when drizzled with colorful herb or chili oils.

6	large dried Chinese mushrooms or other dried mushrooms	6

Marinade:

1/2 tsp	salt	2 mL
1/2 tsp	pepper	2 mL
1 tbsp	dry sherry	15 mL
1 1/2 tsp	cornstarch	7 mL
1 lb	boneless, skinless chicken breast, cut in 1/4-inch (5 mm) dice	500 g
2 oz	bean thread noodles	50 g
1 cup	vegetable oil	250 mL
1	small onion, diced	1
1 cup	diced carrots	250 mL
1 cup	diced celery	250 mL
1	can (6 oz [150 g]) sliced water chestnuts, diced	1
1/4 cup	chicken stock	50 mL
2 tsp	soya sauce	10 mL
1 tbsp	hoisin sauce	15 mL
2 tsp	sesame oil	10 mL
2 tbsp	chopped cilantro	25 mL
12 leaves	iceberg lettuce	12 leaves

1. In a heatproof bowl or pot, cover mushrooms with boiling water and soak for 15 minutes. Drain. Cut off stems and dice caps finely. Set aside.

2. In a bowl, combine ingredients for marinade. Add chicken; mix well to coat. Set aside for 20 minutes.

3. In a nonstick wok or skillet, heat oil over medium-high heat until a piece of noodle dropped into the oil puffs up, turns white and floats to the top instantly. Fry noodles in batches. Drain on paper towel and keep warm. Reserve 1 tbsp (15 mL) oil.

4. In same skillet, heat reserved oil over high heat for 30 seconds. Add onion and chicken and stir-fry for 1 minute. Reduce heat to medium-high; add mushrooms, carrots and celery and stir-fry for 1 minute. Add water chestnuts, chicken stock, soya sauce, hoisin sauce and sesame oil. Cook until vegetables are just tender and liquid is absorbed, about 1 minute. Remove from heat, add cilantro and mix.

5. To Serve: Using kitchen shears or a pair of scissors, cut fried noodles into 1-inch (2.5 cm) strands. Line a large platter with noodles and top with chicken mixture. Arrange lettuce leaves and a small dish of extra hoisin sauce on another platter. Pass both platters around and invite diners to assemble their own wraps by placing a large spoonful of the chicken-noodle mixture and hoisin sauce on a lettuce leaf. Eat open, or rolled up.

PORK AND SHRIMP NOODLE ROLLS

SERVES 6 TO 8

AS AN APPETIZER

In a Chinese restaurant these would be made with steamed rice noodle sheets and filled with shrimp, ground beef or barbecued pork. We've used Vietnamese rice paper which is simple to work with and easier to find.

Steamer, preferably bamboo

6	large dried Chinese mushrooms or other dried mushrooms	6

Marinade:

1/4 tsp	salt	1 mL
1 tbsp	sherry	15 mL
2 tsp	cornstarch	10 mL
4 oz	ground pork	125 g
4 oz	shrimp, chopped	125 g
1 1/2 tsp	vegetable oil	7 mL
2 tsp	minced ginger root	10 mL
1 tsp	red pepper flakes	5 mL
2 cups	shredded Napa cabbage or spinach	500 mL
1 tbsp	oyster sauce	15 mL
1 tsp	soya sauce	5 mL
8	sheets 8-inch (20 cm) round Vietnamese rice paper	8
2 tsp	sesame oil	10 mL
1 tbsp	finely chopped green onions (optional)	15 mL

1. In a heatproof bowl or pot, soak mushrooms in 2 cups (500 mL) boiling water for 15 minutes. Drain, reserving the liquid. Cut off stems and discard. Slice caps into thin strips and set aside.

2. In a bowl, combine ingredients for marinade. Add pork and shrimp, stir to coat and set aside for 10 minutes.

3. In a nonstick wok or skillet, heat oil over medium-high heat for 30 seconds. Add ginger root, red pepper flakes and mushrooms; stir-fry for 1 minute.

Add meat mixture and stir-fry for 1 minute. Add cabbage, mushroom liquid, oyster sauce, and soya sauce. Stir to combine ingredients and cook until the mixture has thickened and liquid is mostly evaporated. Transfer to a bowl and cool.

4. Half-fill a large heatproof bowl or pot with boiling water. Using tongs or chopsticks, immerse one sheet of rice paper in water until it's soft and pliable, about 2 or 3 seconds. Remove sheet, pat dry with a paper towel and place sheet on a flat, dry surface. Spoon 2-3 tbsp (25-45 mL) of the filling onto bottom half of sheet. Fold bottom and side edges over the filling and continue to roll the sheet into a tight cylinder. Place on oiled plate, seam side down, and brush lightly with sesame oil. Repeat until all the filling is used up. This should make eight 6-inch (15 cm) rolls. Rolls can be made a few hours ahead and kept in the refrigerator, covered with a damp towel.

5. Set steamer over boiling water. Place plate with rolls in steamer (or place rolls directly on rack, if you prefer) and steam for 3 minutes. Sprinkle with green onions, if desired. Cut rolls crosswise into bite-sized pieces before serving.

STEAMED BEEF AND CILANTRO BUNDLES

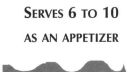

SERVES 6 TO 10

AS AN APPETIZER

We've made these bundles with ground beef but many other fillings — such as prawns with ginger and fish sauce or salmon with scallions and garlic — also come to mind.

Steamer, preferably bamboo

Marinade:

2 tbsp	oyster sauce	25 mL
1 tbsp	soya sauce	15 mL
1 tsp	freshly ground black pepper	5 mL
1 tsp	cornstarch	5 mL
12 oz	extra-lean ground beef	375 g

Bundles:

1 tbsp	vegetable oil	15 mL
1	can (7 oz [175 g]) sliced bamboo shoots, drained and chopped	1
1/2 cup	roasted peanuts	125 mL
1/4 cup	fresh cilantro leaves, finely chopped	50 mL
12	8-inch (20 cm) lengths of green onions (green part only)	12
12	5-inch (12 cm) round sheets Vietnamese rice paper	12

1. In a medium-size bowl combine ingredients for marinade. Add beef, mix well and set aside to marinate for 1 hour.

2. Make the filling: In a nonstick wok or skillet, heat oil over medium-high heat for 30 seconds. Add beef and stir-fry until cooked through, about 3 minutes. Add bamboo shoots and peanuts; stir-fry for 1 minute. Remove from heat and mix in cilantro leaves. Allow to cool.

3. In a large pot of boiling water, blanch green onions until just wilted, about 15 to 20 seconds. Remove and plunge into a bowl of ice water. Drain and set aside.

4. Half-fill a large heatproof bowl or pot with boiling water. Using tongs or chopsticks, immerse a sheet of rice paper in water until it's soft and pliable, about 2 or 3 seconds. Remove sheet, pat dry with a paper towel and lay the sheet on a flat, dry surface. Place 1 heaping tablespoon (15-20 mL) of filling in the center, then gather up the edges of the wrap and tie into a bundle with one of the blanched green onions. Repeat procedure with the remaining ingredients. Bundles can be made a few hours ahead and kept in the refrigerator, covered with a damp towel.

5. Just before serving, place bundles in a preheated, lightly oiled steamer and steam for 2 minutes or until heated through. Serve immediately with Nuoc Cham (see recipe, page 33), chili oil or Tabasco sauce as an accompaniment.

5-SPICE AND MAPLE CURED SALMON ROLL WITH A GINGER-SOY DIPPING SAUCE

SERVES 4

8 oz	5-SPICE AND MAPLE CURED SALMON (see recipe, page 92) *or* lox *or* smoked salmon	250 g
4	8-inch (20 cm) round sheets dried rice paper	4
2 cups	shredded romaine or iceberg lettuce	500 mL
1 cup	bean sprouts	250 mL
1	carrot, peeled and grated	1
2 tbsp	minced fresh basil	25 mL

Dipping Sauce:

1/2 cup	rice vinegar	125 mL
1 tbsp	minced ginger root	15 mL
1 tsp	chili paste	5 mL
1 tbsp	dark soya sauce	15 mL
1 tbsp	brown sugar	15 mL

1. Cut salmon into thin slices (if required). Stack 3 or 4 slices and roll up tightly. With a sharp knife, cut roll into thin shreds. Repeat with remaining salmon.

2. Half-fill a large heatproof bowl or pot with boiling water. Using tongs or chopsticks, immerse one sheet of rice paper in water until it is soft and pliable, about 2 or 3 seconds. Remove sheet and pat dry with a paper towel. Place sheet on a flat, dry surface.

3. Cover rice paper with one quarter of the salmon slices. Top salmon with one quarter of the lettuce, the sprouts, the carrot and the basil. Fold ends and side edge over the filling and roll into a tight cylinder. The rice paper should stick together in a smooth surface. Repeat procedure with remaining sheets.

4. Make the sauce: In a small bowl, combine the rice vinegar, ginger, chili paste, soya sauce and sugar. Set aside.

5. Cut each roll in half and serve with dipping sauce.

SOUPS

CRAB DUMPLINGS IN BROTH

SERVES 4 TO 6

AS A STARTER

This delicate soup makes a wonderful introduction to an elegant meal. Dried shrimp is available in Asian markets and gives the broth a nice kick, but use it sparingly as it has a tendency to overpower other flavors.

Filling:

4	large Napa cabbage leaves	4
8 oz	cooked crabmeat, finely chopped	250 g
1 tbsp	minced ginger root	15 mL
1 tsp	sesame oil	5 mL
1/4 tsp	white pepper	1 mL
2 tsp	fish sauce	10 mL
1	egg, beaten	1
20	wonton wrappers	20

Broth:

5 cups	chicken stock	1.25 L
1 tbsp	dried shrimp (optional)	15 mL
	Salt and freshly ground black pepper, to taste	
2 tbsp	chopped yellow Chinese chives *or* green onions	25 mL

1. In a large pot of boiling water, blanch Napa cabbage leaves for 2 minutes. Drain and plunge into a bowl of ice water to stop cooking. When cool, drain and pat dry with paper towels. Cut leaves into thin strands.

2. In a mixing bowl, combine cabbage with remaining filling ingredients; mix well. Adjust amount of fish sauce to suit your taste. (This will depend on saltiness of the crabmeat.)

3. On a work surface, lay out one wonton wrapper. Place 1 tbsp (15 mL) of filling in the center; brush edges with beaten egg and fold diagonally over filling to seal tightly. Crimp the edges by pressing down gently with your fingers while making a few small folds in the sealed edge of wrapper. Dumplings can be kept in refrigerator overnight, covered with a lightly dampened towel.

4. Just before serving, bring a large pot of water to a boil. Add dumplings and cook until they float to the surface. Remove with a slotted spoon and place in a large serving bowl or soup tureen.

5. Meanwhile, in a medium-sized pot, bring stock and dried shrimp to a boil. Cover and cook for 2 minutes. Season with salt and pepper to taste, then pour hot broth over dumplings. Garnish with chopped chives and serve immediately.

CURRY-FRIED TOFU SOUP WITH VEGETABLES AND UDON NOODLES

SERVES 4

We recommend that you make the effort to find Madras curry powder for this recipe. (Look for it in Asian markets.) Rusty in color and usually containing bay leaves, it is fuller and more complex than regular curry powder, which contains more turmeric and tends to be bitter.

Bouquet Garni:

3	slices ginger root	3
1	garlic clove	1
1	stalk lemon grass, smashed and sliced *or* 1 tbsp (15 mL) lemon zest	1
2	star anise	2
2	thumb-sized pieces of dried tangerine peel, rinsed, *or* 2 tsp (10 mL) orange zest	2

Soup:

6 cups	vegetable or chicken stock	1.5 L
1	package (1 lb [500 g]) medium-firm tofu	1
2 tbsp	Madras curry powder	25 mL
1/4 tsp	salt	1 mL
4	packages (7 oz [200 g]) udon noodles *or* 1 lb (500 g) fresh spaghetti	4
2 cups	bean sprouts	500 mL
2 tbsp	vegetable oil	25 mL
1 cup	carrots, cut into matchsticks	250 mL
2 cups	broccoli florets	500 mL
1/2 tsp	salt	2 mL
4 sprigs	cilantro	4 sprigs

1. Wrap ingredients for *bouquet garni* in a piece of cheesecloth and tie securely with kitchen twine.

2. In a large saucepan or stock pot over high heat, bring bouquet garni and stock to a boil. Lower heat to medium and cook for 3 minutes. Cover and allow to steep for 15 minutes. Remove *bouquet garni*.

3. Cut tofu into 2-inch (5 cm) squares, about 1/2 inch (1 cm) thick. Pat dry with paper towels. In a mixing bowl, combine curry powder and salt; dredge tofu in mixture until lightly but evenly coated.

4. In a large pot of boiling salted water, cook noodles until *al dente*, about 2 minutes. Drain and divide between 4 serving bowls. Top with equally divided portions of bean sprouts.

5. In a nonstick wok or skillet, heat oil over medium-high heat for 30 seconds. Add tofu and fry until golden brown and slightly crisp on the outside, about 1 minute per side.

6. Meanwhile, bring broth to a boil. Add carrots and broccoli and cook until vegetables are just tender, about 3 minutes. Season with salt. Pour boiling broth and vegetables over noodle mixture. Top with tofu. Garnish with cilantro and serve immediately.

VIETNAMESE-STYLE BEEF NOODLE SOUP

SERVES 4

AS A MAIN COURSE OR

6 AS A STARTER

A variation on the famous Vietnamese Pho, *this is a great way to use up leftover roasts, including pork or lamb.*

8 oz	thin vermicelli (thin rice stick) noodles *or* dried angel hair pasta	250 g
	Vegetable oil for coating noodles	

Broth:

6 cups	beef stock	1.5 L
1	stalk lemon grass, smashed and cut into 4-inch (10 cm) lengths *or* 1 tbsp (15 mL) lemon zest	1
3	slices ginger root, smashed	3
1/2 tsp	HOME-STYLE 5-SPICE MIX (see recipe, page 28) *or* commercially prepared 5-spice powder (optional)	2 mL
1	small onion, thinly sliced	1
1	clove garlic, thinly sliced	1
1 tbsp	fish sauce	15 mL
	Freshly ground black pepper, to taste	
2 cups	bean sprouts	500 mL
1 cup	watercress leaves (optional)	250 mL
12 oz	thinly sliced roast beef	375 g
2 tbsp	thinly sliced fresh basil leaves	25 mL
1 or 2	red chilies, thinly sliced crosswise	1 or 2
1	lime, quartered	1

1. In a heatproof bowl or pot, cover noodles with boiling water and soak for 3 minutes. (If using pasta, prepare according to package directions.) Drain, coat with a little oil and set aside.

2. In a large saucepan, bring stock to a boil. Add lemon grass, ginger root and 5-SPICE MIX (if using); reduce heat to medium; cover and cook for 3 minutes.

3. With a slotted spoon, remove lemon grass and ginger root. Add onion and garlic; bring to a boil and cook for 1 minute. Season with fish sauce and pepper.

4. Meanwhile, divide noodles into 4 large soup bowls. Top each with one quarter of the bean sprouts, the watercress leaves and the beef slices. Garnish with basil and chilies. Pour boiling broth over noodle mixture and serve with wedges of lime to squeeze over soup.

Chicken and Tomato Soup with Glass Noodle Egg Drop Dumplings

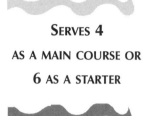

SERVES 4

AS A MAIN COURSE OR

6 AS A STARTER

Marinade:

2 tsp	minced ginger root	10 mL
1 tbsp	dry sherry *or* white wine	15 mL
1/4 tsp	salt	1 mL
1 tbsp	soya sauce	15 mL
2 tsp	cornstarch	10 mL
8 oz	boneless chicken breast, cut into thin strips 2 inches (5 cm) long	250 g
2 oz	bean thread noodles *or* angel hair pasta	50 g
2	large eggs, beaten	2

Broth:

6 cups	chicken stock	1.5 L
3	large tomatoes, peeled, seeded and coarsely chopped	3
1	small onion, sliced	1
1/2	English cucumber, cut into 2-inch (5 cm) long matchsticks *or* 1 cup (250 mL) fresh or frozen peas	1/2
	Salt and white pepper, to taste	
2 tbsp	coarsely chopped cilantro leaves	25 mL

1. In a bowl, combine ingredients for marinade. Add chicken and set aside for 20 minutes.

2. In a heatproof bowl or pot, cover noodles with boiling water and soak for 3 minutes. (If using pasta, prepare according to package directions.) Drain and chop into 1/2-inch (1 cm) lengths.

3. In a medium-sized bowl whisk eggs. Add noodle pieces, mix well and set aside.

4. In a large pot, combine chicken stock, tomatoes and onion; bring to a boil. Reduce heat to low, cover and simmer for 15 minutes. Add chicken and return to a boil. Simmer for 2 minutes or until chicken is cooked. Bring mixture back to a rolling boil and slowly pour noodle mixture into the soup, stirring vigorously. Add cucumber and cook for 1 minute to warm through. Season with salt and white pepper, garnish with chopped cilantro and serve immediately.

Shrimp and Cottage Cheese Dumplings in Clamato Broth

Serves 4

AS A MAIN COURSE OR

6 AS A STARTER

Filling:

4 oz	raw shrimp, peeled, deveined and coarsely chopped	125 g
1 cup	cottage cheese	250 mL
1/2 tsp	freshly ground black pepper	2 mL
2 tbsp	chopped green onions	25 mL
24	round Chinese dumpling wrappers	24
1	large egg, beaten	1

Broth:

2 cups	clamato juice	500 mL
3 cups	chicken stock	750 mL
3	slices ginger root, 1/4 inch (5 mm) thick	3
1/2	medium red onion, chopped	1/2
1/2 cup	chopped carrots	125 mL
1/2 cup	chopped celery	125 mL
	Salt and pepper to taste	
2 tbsp	cilantro leaves	25 mL

1. In small bowl, combine ingredients for filling; mix well.

2. On a flat, dry surface, lay out one dumpling wrapper. Place 1/2 tbsp (7 mL) of filling in the center, brush the edges with egg and cover with another wrapper. Press gently with fingers to squeeze the air out and seal the edges. Repeat until all the filling is used up, using additional wrappers, if necessary.

3. In a medium-sized saucepan, bring clamato juice and stock to a boil. Add ginger root, onion, carrots and celery; return to a boil. Skim off any froth that floats to the top. Cook for 2 minutes or until vegetables are tender. Remove ginger root, season with salt and pepper and keep warm.

4. In a large pot of boiling salted water, cook dumplings for 2 minutes. Using a slotted spoon, transfer to individual bowls. Pour hot soup over dumplings, sprinkle with cilantro and serve immediately.

ASSORTED MEATS AND SEAFOOD WITH UDON IN MISO SOUP

SERVES 4

This recipe makes a quick and delicious lunch. We've used barbecued pork, which you can buy in Chinatown, but it works equally well with other cooked meats such as roast beef.

5 cups	chicken stock	1.25 L
2 tbsp	red *miso* paste	25 mL
1 tsp	sesame oil	5 mL
3	slices ginger root, 1/4 inch (5 mm) thick	3
12 oz	udon noodles *or* any long-tubed pasta such as ziti or macaroni	350 g
4 oz	barbecued pork, sliced	125 g
2	hard-boiled eggs, halved	2
4	stems Chinese broccoli *or* broccoli *or* rapini *or* bok choy, cut into 2-inch (5 cm) lengths	4
8	large shrimp, shelled and deveined	8
6	large scallops, cut crosswise in 3 slices	6
	Salt to taste	
1 tsp	Japanese 7-spice or coarsely ground black pepper	5 mL

1. In a large saucepan or soup pot, combine chicken stock, *miso* paste, sesame oil and ginger root slices; bring to a boil. Cook for 1 minute. Add noodles and cook until *al dente*. (Check package instructions.) Using a slotted spoon, transfer noodles or pasta to a soup tureen or 4 bowls. Arrange pork slices and eggs on top.

2. Add broccoli to broth; bring to boil and cook for 1 minute. Add seafood, return to boil and continue cooking for 1 minute. Season with salt. Ladle soup mixture over noodles, sprinkle with 7-spice or pepper and serve immediately.

RAMEN NOODLE SOUP WITH RED SNAPPER, SPINACH AND GARLIC

SERVES 2 TO 4

Little square packs of instant ramen noodles with various flavorings are available almost everywhere. With a little effort, they can be quickly transformed into a special meal.

This recipe works well with vegetable, chicken and seafood flavorings.

The spinach can be replaced with kale, broccoli or cabbage.

8 oz	red snapper fillets, or any other firm white fish	250 g

Broth:

4 cups	water	1 L
1 tsp	minced garlic	5 mL
2	packages ramen soup noodles, with seasoning	2
4 oz	fresh spinach, finely chopped	125 g
1 tsp	chopped cilantro	5 mL
1 tsp	sesame oil	5 mL
	Hot sauce to taste	

1. Remove any skin or bones from fish. Cut into 1/2-inch (1 cm) cubes and set aside.

2. In a large pot, bring water to a boil. Add fish and garlic and return to a boil. Add noodles, reduce heat and simmer for 3 minutes or until noodles are soft. Add seasoning packet, spinach, cilantro, sesame oil and hot sauce; stir gently. Ladle soup into 4 bowls and serve immediately.

MUSSELS IN A SPICED TOMATO BROTH WITH BEAN THREAD NOODLES

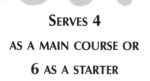

SERVES 4

AS A MAIN COURSE OR

6 AS A STARTER

This dish is a wonderful mixture of Indonesian spices and mussels in a complex tomato broth. Try cooking it in a Chinese sand hotpot and serve from the container along with a loaf of crusty sourdough bread.

2 oz	bean thread noodles *or* angel hair pasta	50 g
1 tbsp	vegetable oil, plus oil for coating noodles	15 mL

Broth:

1	onion, finely diced	1
1 tbsp	minced garlic	15 mL
1 tbsp	minced ginger root	15 mL
1 tsp	dried coriander seeds	5 mL
1 tsp	dried anise seeds	5 mL
1 tsp	mustard seeds	5 mL
1	cinnamon stick (or 1 tsp [5 mL] ground cinnamon)	1
1	stalk lemon grass, coarsely chopped *or* 1 tbsp (15 mL) lemon zest	1
4 cups	tomato juice	1 L
2 cups	chicken or vegetable stock *or* clam juice	500 mL
	Hot pepper sauce to taste	
	Salt and pepper to taste	
2 lb	fresh mussels	1 kg
	Chopped cilantro to taste	

1. In a heatproof bowl or pot, cover noodles with boiling water and soak for 3 minutes. Drain. (If using pasta, prepare according to package directions, drain and coat with a little oil.) Set aside.

2. In a large pot, heat oil over medium-high heat for 30 seconds. Add onion and cook until it softens and begins to change color. Add garlic and ginger root; sauté for 1 minute. Add coriander, anise and mustard seeds; toss while heating through to release flavors.

3. Add cinnamon, lemon grass, tomato juice and stock or clam juice; bring mixture to a boil. Reduce heat and simmer for 15 minutes. Season to taste with hot pepper sauce, salt and pepper. If possible, allow mixture to stand for 30 minutes to develop flavor. Strain broth through a fine mesh strainer and return to pot.

4. Bring broth back to a boil. Add mussels and noodles; cook until the mussels open. (Discard any that don't open.) Remove from heat and transfer to 4 warm bowls. Sprinkle with chopped cilantro and serve.

SHREDDED CHICKEN, MUSHROOM AND EGG NOODLE SOUP

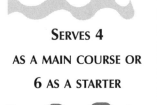

SERVES 4

AS A MAIN COURSE OR

6 AS A STARTER

*Chicken soup is known
as a great comfort food
and this recipe — which
produces a nourishing
and satisfying meal —
lives up to that standard.*

*You can use leftover
chicken, but for the best
results use a good stock.*

1 tbsp	vegetable oil	15 mL
1	onion, thinly sliced	1
1 tbsp	minced garlic	15 mL
1 cup	sliced mushrooms	250 mL
1	carrot, peeled and grated	1
1 tbsp	hoisin sauce	15 mL
1 cup	shredded cooked chicken	250 mL
6 cups	chicken stock	1.5 L
1 cup	thin dried egg noodles, crushed	250 mL
1 tsp	sesame oil	5 mL
1	sliced green onion	1
	Salt and pepper to taste	

1. In a large saucepan, heat oil over medium-high heat for 30 seconds. Add onion and cook until it softens and begins to change color. Add garlic, mushrooms and carrot; sauté for 1 minute. Add hoisin sauce, chicken, stock and noodles; stir until well mixed.

2. Bring mixture to a boil; reduce heat and simmer for 5 minutes or until the noodles are soft. Season with salt and pepper to taste. Drizzle with sesame oil and garnish with green onion. Serve immediately.

RICE NOODLE SALAD WITH SUGAR SNAP PEAS, SWEET PEPPERS AND ALMONDS (PAGE 85) ➤

OVERLEAF: MUSSELS IN A SPICED TOMATO BROTH WITH BEAN THREAD NOODLES (PAGE 62) ➤

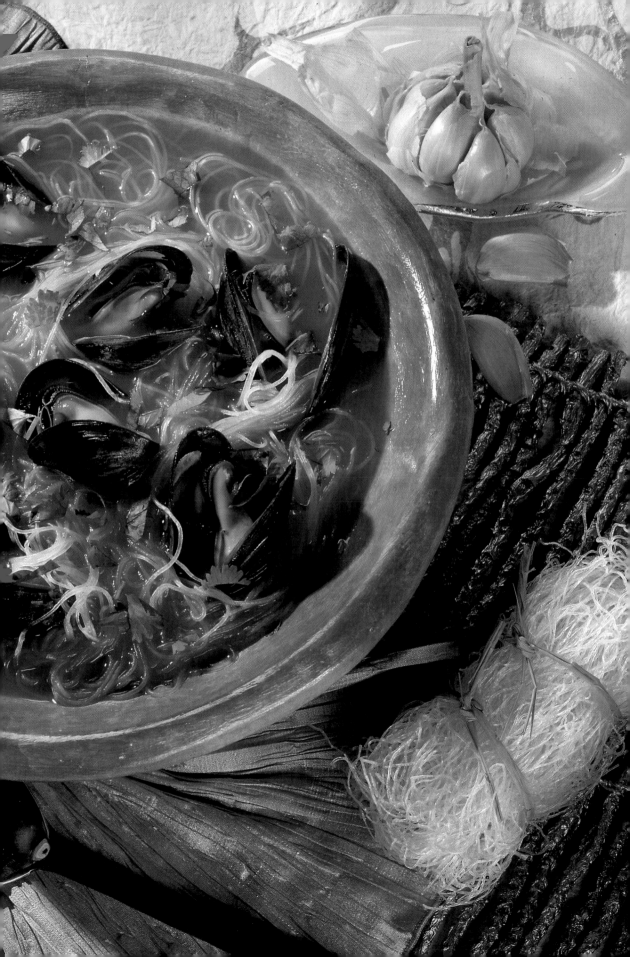

Spicy Salmon Bundles in a Ginger and Lettuce Broth

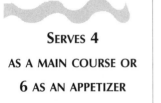

Serves 4

as a main course or

6 as an appetizer

*These delicious bundles
can be made with any
type of salmon — even
canned salmon (drained
of oil or juice) in a pinch.*

*Once prepared, the
wontons must be han-
dled delicately. If the
mixture is wet, the wrap-
per will become soggy
and tear easily.*

4 oz	salmon, finely diced	125 g
1	whole green onion, finely chopped	1
1 tbsp	minced ginger root	15 mL
2	water chestnuts, minced	2
1 tbsp	finely chopped cilantro	15 mL
1 tsp	sesame oil	5 mL
1 tsp	Tabasco or other hot sauce	5 mL
24	wonton wrappers	24
1	egg mixed with 1 tbsp (15 mL) water	1
6 cups	chicken or vegetable stock	1.5 L
1 tbsp	minced ginger root	15 mL
1 tsp	minced garlic	5 mL
1 cup	shredded iceberg lettuce	250 mL
1 tbsp	finely chopped cilantro	15 mL
	Salt and pepper to taste	

1. In a small bowl, combine salmon, green onion, ginger root, water chestnuts, cilantro, sesame oil and
   hot sauce. Mix well.

2. On a work surface, lay out 4 wrappers and brush
   with a liberal amount of the egg and water mixture.
   Place 1 tsp (5 mL) of filling in the center of each and
   bring the sides up to form a small bundle. Grab the
   top and give it a gentle twist to seal the package.
   Repeat with remaining filling and wrappers

3. In a large saucepan, combine stock, ginger root and
   garlic; bring to a boil. Reduce heat and simmer for 5
   minutes. Add bundles and simmer for 3 minutes.
   Gently fold in lettuce and heat through, about 1 or 2
   minutes. Season with salt and pepper to taste.
   Transfer to bowls and garnish with chopped cilantro.

◄ Moo Shu-Style Prawns with Spinach Noodles (page 100)

JULIENNE ROOT VEGETABLE SOUP WITH RICE STICK NOODLES AND A MINT-BASIL PESTO

SERVES 4

The pesto used here is a simple paste made from fresh herbs and oil with added seasonings. It's a quick and easy way to inject flavor into any dish. For a thicker paste, add peanuts before puréeing.

Pesto:

1 cup	basil leaves	250 mL
1 cup	mint leaves	250 mL
1 tbsp	chopped garlic	15 mL
1/4 cup	vegetable oil	50 mL
	Salt and pepper to taste	
1/4 cup	unsalted peanuts (optional)	50 mL

Broth:

6 cups	vegetable or chicken stock	1.5 L
1	carrot, peeled and julienned	1
1	small yam, peeled and julienned	1
1	parsnip, peeled and julienned	1
1	onion, thinly sliced	1
4 oz	broad vermicelli (broad rice stick noodles)	125 g
	Salt and pepper to taste	

1. In a blender or food processor, purée basil, mint, garlic and oil to the consistency of a smooth paste. Peanuts, if used, will thicken the mixture into a firmer paste. Season with salt and pepper. Set aside.

2. In a large saucepan or soup pot, combine stock, carrot, yam, parsnip and onion; bring to a boil. Reduce heat and simmer 5 minutes. Add noodles and cook until noodles are soft and the vegetables are tender, about 5 minutes. Season with salt and pepper.

3. Ladle the soup into 4 bowls and top with a generous spoonful of pesto. Pass the remaining pesto at the table.

5-SPICE MAPLE-CURED SALMON AND RICE VERMICELLI SOUP

SERVES 4

This is a quick, easy and delicious soup which also works well with shredded salmon or cod. For best results, add the raw fish to the boiling hot broth just before serving.

1 tbsp	vegetable oil	15 mL
1 tbsp	minced ginger root	15 mL
1	carrot, peeled and grated	1
6 cups	fish or chicken stock *or* clam juice	1.5 L
4 oz	rice vermicelli (rice stick noodles) broad or thin	125 g
1 cup	shredded *sui choy* or Napa cabbage	250 mL
1 tsp	sesame oil	5 mL
4 oz	5-SPICE MAPLE-CURED SALMON (see recipe, page 92) *or* lox *or* smoked salmon, shredded	125 g
1 tbsp	chopped cilantro	15 mL
	Salt and pepper to taste	

1. In a large saucepan, heat oil over medium-high heat for 30 seconds. Add ginger root and carrot and sauté for 1 minute. Add, stock, noodles, *sui choy* and stir.

2. Bring mixture to a boil. Reduce heat and simmer for 3 minutes or until the noodles are soft. Season with salt and pepper to taste and drizzle with sesame oil.

3. Ladle soup into 4 bowls. Garnish with shredded salmon and cilantro. Serve immediately.

Hot-and-Sour Soup with Sliced Pork, Napa Cabbage and Flat Rice Noodles

Serves 4

AS A MAIN COURSE OR

6 AS A STARTER

8	small dried Chinese mushrooms or other dried mushrooms	8

Marinade:

2 tbsp	fish sauce	25 mL
1 tsp	freshly ground black pepper	5 mL
1 tbsp	sherry	15 mL
2 tsp	cornstarch	10 mL
12 oz	lean pork, thinly sliced	375 g
1 lb	fresh flat rice noodles *or* 8 oz (250 g) broad dried vermicelli (broad rice stick noodles)	500 g
	Oil for coating dried noodles	

Broth:

3 cups	chicken stock	750 mL
2	star anise	2
5	leaves fresh sage (or 1/2 tsp [2 mL] dried)	5
3 cups	sliced Napa cabbage	750 mL
1/2 cup	cider vinegar	125 mL
2-3 tsp	sugar	10-15 mL
1 to 2	small red chilies, seeded and sliced	1 to 2
2 tbsp	fish sauce (or to taste)	25 mL
2 cups	bean sprouts	500 mL
2 tbsp	chopped green onions	25 mL

1. In a heatproof bowl or pot, soak mushrooms in 2 cups (500 mL) boiling water for 15 minutes. Drain and reserve liquid. Cut off mushrooms stems and discard. Set caps aside.

2. In a small bowl, combine ingredients for marinade. Add pork, mix well and set aside to marinate for 20 minutes.

3. If using fresh noodles, separate them just before serving by placing them in a colander under running hot water. (If necessary use your hands to separate the noodles.) If using dried noodles, place them in a heatproof bowl or pot, and cover with boiling water; soak for 5 minutes. Drain. Divide noodles among soup bowls.

4. In a large nonreactive (or nonstick) saucepan, combine mushroom liquid, chicken stock, star anise and sage leaves. Bring to a boil over medium-high heat. Add mushrooms, cover and cook for 2 minutes. Remove star anise and sage, if desired. Add pork and Napa cabbage; bring to a boil and cook for 3 minutes; skim off any froth that floats to the top. Add vinegar, 2 tsp (10 mL) of the sugar and the chilies; cook for 1 minute. Season with fish sauce and additional sugar, if desired.

5. Remove pot from heat, add bean sprouts and green onions; stir. Ladle portions of broth and vegetables over noodles and serve immediately.

ROAST BEEF, GARLIC AND ONIONS WITH HOT-AND-SOUR RAMEN SOUP

SERVES 4

Another in our repertoire of quick and easy soups, this can be made in little more than the time it takes to boil the water.

4 oz	sliced, cooked roast beef, shredded	125 g
2	packages ramen noodles, flavor packet discarded	2
1 tbsp	minced garlic	15 mL
1	onion, sliced	1
1 tsp	hot pepper sauce	5 mL
6 cups	beef stock	1.5 L
1 tsp	sesame oil	5 mL
1 tbsp	rice vinegar	15 mL
1 tbsp	soya sauce	15 mL
1 cup	bean sprouts	250 mL
	Salt and pepper to taste	

1. In a large saucepan, heat oil over medium-high heat for 30 seconds. Add ginger root and onion and sauté until onion wilts and begins to change color. Add stock and noodles; stir.

2. Bring mixture to a boil; reduce heat and simmer for 3 to 4 minutes or until the noodles are soft. Season with salt and pepper to taste. Add sesame oil, rice vinegar and soya sauce; stir to mix.

3. Ladle mixture into 4 bowls. Garnish with shredded beef and bean sprouts. Serve immediately.

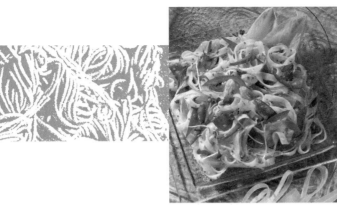

*S*ALADS

RICE STICK NOODLE AND CARROT SALAD WITH A CURRIED GINGER AND COCONUT MILK DRESSING

SERVES 4

Rice noodles and coconut milk are a popular combination in southeast Asia.

If fresh herbs are available, toss in some basil, mint, coriander or chives.

The curry paste is worth the effort, as uncooked curry powder has a tendency to be bitter.

For a more festive salad, use this as a base and top with cooked seafood.

8 oz	dried broad vermicelli (rice stick noodles) *or* angel hair pasta	250 g
	Vegetable oil for coating noodles	
1	can (14 oz [400 mL]) homogenized coconut milk	1
1 tbsp	curry paste *or* curry powder	15 mL
1 tbsp	minced ginger root	15 mL
2 tbsp	rice vinegar	25 mL
2 cups	grated carrots	500 mL
	Hot pepper sauce, to taste	
	Large handful of fresh bean sprouts (optional)	
	Handful of roasted peanuts (optional)	

1. In a heatproof bowl or pot, cover noodles with boiling water and soak for 5 minutes. (If using pasta, prepare according to package directions.) Drain, coat with a little vegetable oil and set aside in a mixing bowl.

2. In a medium-sized bowl, combine coconut milk, curry paste, ginger root, rice vinegar, carrots and hot sauce. Mix well and pour over noodles. Refrigerate for at least 1 hour to allow flavors to develop. Transfer to a serving bowl and garnish with bean sprouts and/or peanuts, if desired.

COLD SOBA NOODLE SALAD WITH A SOYA AND MUSTARD DRESSING

SERVES 8

This dish echoes that Japanese favorite, ice cold soba noodles dipped in a wasabi and soya sauce. If you dress the salad just before serving, the noodles will have the firm texture the Japanese love.

Marinating overnight will produce a softer noodle and a more integrated flavor. A sprinkling of shredded nori seaweed and toasted sesame seeds make a wonderful finish.

1 lb	dried soba noodles *or* wholewheat linguine	500 g
1 tsp	sesame oil	5 mL

Dressing:

1 tbsp	Dijon mustard	15 mL
1 tbsp	soya sauce	15 mL
1 tbsp	water	15 mL
1 cup	vegetable oil	250 mL
1 tbsp	minced ginger root	15 mL
1 tsp	hot pepper sauce, or to taste	5 mL

Salt and pepper to taste

Nori (sushi seaweed sheets), optional

Sesame seeds for garnish

1. In a large pot of boiling salted water cook the noodles until *al dente*, about 7 to 8 minutes. (If using pasta, prepare according to package directions.) Drain, rinse with cold water and toss with sesame oil.

2. Make the dressing: Put mustard, soya sauce, water, oil, ginger root and hot pepper sauce in a blender; blend at low speed until smooth. Season to taste with salt and pepper.

3. In a serving bowl, combine noodles and dressing. Toss well to mix and garnish with *nori* and/or sesame seeds.

RICE WRAP NOODLE SALAD WITH BARBECUED DUCK

SERVES 4

For an interesting variation, try adding fruits such as pineapple chunks or fresh peaches.

You can substitute vegetables such as celery and cucumbers for the snow peas (they don't require blanching).

If you can find them, use soya bean sprouts with the yellow seeds attached.

Roast chicken or turkey can be used instead of the duck.

Dressing:

2 tbsp	fresh lime juice	25 mL
1 tbsp	fish sauce	15 mL
1 tbsp	soya sauce	15 mL
1 tbsp	sesame oil	15 mL
2	red chilies, seeded and finely chopped	2
2 tsp	minced garlic	10 mL
1 tbsp	thinly sliced pickled ginger root (optional)	15 mL
1 tbsp	pickling liquid from ginger (optional)	15 mL

Salad:

3 cups	bean sprouts	750 mL
8 oz	snow peas, trimmed	250 mL
20	sheets Vietnamese rice paper	20
2 cups	Chinese barbecued duck meat, shredded	500 mL
1	large red bell pepper, seeded and cut into matchsticks	1
1/2 cup	cilantro leaves	125 mL
1/3 cup	coarsely chopped roasted peanuts	75 mL

1. In a nonreactive (or ceramic) bowl, combine all dressing ingredients; mix well and set aside for 20 minutes to develop flavors.

2. Meanwhile, in a colander, rinse bean sprouts under cold water. Transfer to a mixing bowl and soak in ice water for at least 10 minutes. Drain well just before use.

3. In a large pot of boiling salted water, blanch snow peas for 1 minute. Drain and plunge peas immediately into ice water to stop cooking. When thoroughly cooled, drain and set aside.

4. To make rice wrap noodles, dip pieces of rice paper, a few at a time, in near-boiling water for 5 to 10 seconds, until soft. Quickly gather rice paper into a loose roll and cut the roll crosswise into segments 1/3-inch (7 mm) wide. Unroll and place in a serving bowl. Repeat procedure with remaining sheets, then fluff the noodles to separate them.

5. In a serving bowl, top noodles with bean sprouts, snow peas, bell pepper, duck meat, cilantro and peanuts. Sprinkle with dressing. Toss well and serve.

EGG NOODLES IN QUICK PEANUT SAUCE WITH WATER CHESTNUT SALAD

SERVES 4

If you can find it, use jicama in place of the water chestnuts; it adds a wonderfully nutty taste to the dish.

Peanut Sauce:

1 tbsp	hoisin sauce	15 mL
1/2 tbsp	hot bean sauce	7 mL
2 tsp	minced ginger root	10 mL
1 tsp	minced garlic	5 mL
2/3 cup	unsalted peanut butter	175 mL
2 tbsp	vegetable or chicken stock, warmed	25 mL
1 tbsp	lemon juice, or to taste	15 mL

Dressing:

1 tbsp	sugar (or to taste)	15 mL
2 tbsp	fish sauce	25 mL
3 tbsp	fresh lime juice	45 mL
1 tbsp	cider vinegar	15 mL
12 oz	dried medium egg noodles	375 g

Salad:

2 cups	water chestnuts *or* jicama, cut in matchsticks	500 mL
1 cup	cucumber, cut in matchsticks	250 mL
1 cup	carrots, cut in matchsticks	250 mL
1/4 cup	chopped fresh mint	50 mL
1/4 cup	chopped cilantro	50 mL

1. In a small bowl, whisk together peanut sauce ingredients except stock and lemon juice. Add stock slowly and stir vigorously until mixture has consistency of a smooth, thick sauce. Adjust with lemon juice to taste.

2. In a small bowl, combine ingredients for dressing. Set aside for 10 minutes to blend flavors.

3. In a large pot of boiling salted water, cook noodles until *al dente*. Drain and transfer to a mixing bowl. Add peanut sauce and toss. Refrigerate until well chilled.

4. In a large bowl, toss salad ingredients with dressing. Arrange chilled noodles on plates; top with salad.

THIN WHEAT NOODLES WITH SHREDDED DUCK, BEAN SPROUTS AND A 5-SPICE VINAIGRETTE

SERVES 6

Chinese barbecue duck is a wonderful take-out treat, but chicken makes a great substitute.

Duck can be fatty so remove as much fat as possible when shredding the meat.

For some extra crunch, add thinly sliced raw cabbage.

Vinaigrette:

1/2 cup	rice vinegar	125 mL
2 tbsp	hoisin sauce	25 mL
1 tbsp	prepared mustard such as Dijon	15 mL
1 tsp	HOME-STYLE 5-SPICE MIX (see recipe, page 28) *or* commercially prepared 5-spice powder	5 mL
1 tbsp	minced ginger root	15 mL
2 tbsp	water	25 mL
1 cup	vegetable oil	250 mL

Salad:

1 lb	fresh thin wheat noodles *or* fresh fettuccine	500 g
1 cup	shredded barbecue duck *or* roast chicken	250 mL
1	carrot, peeled and grated	1
2 cups	bean sprouts	500 mL
1/4 cup	roasted peanuts	50 mL

1. In a large bowl, combine rice vinegar, hoisin sauce, mustard, 5-SPICE MIX and water; mix well. Using a whisk, stir continuously while adding the oil in a steady stream. Set vinaigrette aside.

2. In a large pot of boiling salted water, cook noodles until *al dente*, about 4 to 5 minutes. (If using pasta, prepare according to package directions.) Drain, coat with a little vegetable oil and toss well.

3. In a large bowl, combine noodles, duck, carrots, sprouts and dressing. Mix well. Divide mixture between 4 bowls (or place on a large serving platter), top with roasted peanuts and serve.

MARINATED MUSHROOM AND CRISPY CHOW MEIN SALAD

SERVES 4

This is a great make-ahead salad.

Fresh button mushrooms can be used on their own, but varieties such as oyster, shiitake or portobello mushrooms will add some zest.

Use a pair of kitchen shears to break up the crispy chow mein.

Preheat oven to 375° F (190° F)

10-inch (22 cm) ovenproof frying pan (or cast iron skillet) or 9- by 13-inch (3 L) baking dish

2 tbsp	vegetable oil, plus oil for coating noodles	25 mL
1 lb	assorted mushrooms	500 g
1 cup	rice vinegar	250 mL
2 tbsp	honey	25 mL
2 tbsp	minced garlic	25 mL
1 tbsp	cilantro	15 mL
2 tbsp	sweet soya sauce	25 mL
1 tbsp	red chili sauce	15 mL
1 tsp	sesame oil	5 mL
4	whole green onions, thinly sliced	4
1 tbsp	vegetable oil	15 mL
1 lb	fresh chow mein noodles	500 g
1 tbsp	toasted sesame seeds	15 mL

1. Prepare mushrooms by wiping clean with a cloth and slicing off any hard stems. If using oyster mushrooms, break up the clumps. Leave smaller mushroom whole and slice larger ones into bite-size pieces.

2. In a pot of boiling salted water, blanch mushrooms for 3 minutes. Drain and set aside until cool.

3. In a medium-sized bowl, combine vinegar, honey, garlic, cilantro, soya sauce, chili paste and sesame oil. Add mushrooms and toss to coat.

4. In a heatproof bowl or pot, cover noodles with boiling water and soak for 5 minutes. Drain and toss with half the green onions and a little vegetable oil.

5. In a nonstick skillet, ovenproof if possible, heat oil over medium heat for 30 seconds. Add noodle mixture and cook, shaking the pan occasionally, until the noodles become golden brown, about 10 minutes. With a fork, gently fluff noodles. Place pan in pre-heated oven (or transfer to baking dish, if using) and bake until noodles are crisp and browned, about 15 minutes. Set aside until cool, then break into small chunks.

6. In a large serving bowl, combine noodles and mushroom mixture; toss well. Garnish with green onions and sesame seeds.

BROAD EGG NOODLE AND VEGETABLE SALAD WITH A SPICY BLACK BEAN VINAIGRETTE

SERVES 4

If you're too impatient to whisk this robust vinaigrette by hand, use a blender. Just add the oil in a steady stream.

The dressing also works well with any green salad. But make sure you add green vegetables just before serving — otherwise they'll turn a drab and unappealing shade of green.

Vinaigrette:

1 tbsp	dark soya sauce	15 mL
1/2 cup	rice vinegar	125 mL
2 tbsp	black bean sauce	25 mL
2 tbsp	honey	25 mL
1 tbsp	prepared mustard, such as Dijon	15 mL
1 tsp	chili paste	5 tsp
2 tbsp	water	25 mL
1 cup	vegetable oil	250 mL

Salad:

1 lb	fresh broad egg noodles *or* 8 oz (250 g) dried fettuccine *or* linguine	500 g
1 tbsp	vegetable oil	15 mL
1	carrot, peeled and thinly sliced	1
1 tbsp	minced ginger root	15 mL
1 tbsp	minced garlic	15 mL
2 cups	thinly sliced Chinese broccoli *or* broccoli	500 mL
2 cups	shredded Chinese cabbage *or* green cabbage	500 mL
2	whole green onions, thinly sliced	2

1. In a large bowl, combine soya sauce, vinegar, black bean sauce, honey, mustard, chili paste and water; add oil in a steady stream, whisking constantly to emulsify. Set aside.

2. If using fresh noodles, cut into 4-inch (10 cm) strips. (If using dried pasta, break strands in half.)

3. In a large pot of boiling salted water, cook noodles until *al dente*, about 4 to 5 minutes. (If using pasta, prepare according to package directions.) Drain, coat with a little oil and set aside.

4. In a nonstick wok or skillet, heat oil over high for 30 seconds. Add carrots, ginger root and garlic. Sauté for 2 to 3 minutes. Add broccoli and cook until tender, about 2 minutes. Season with salt and pepper and remove from heat.

5. In a large bowl, combine vinaigrette, noodles, vegetable mixture and Chinese cabbage; toss. Garnish with green onions and serve immediately.

SHREDDED CHICKEN SALAD WITH SPICY SESAME VINAIGRETTE

SERVES 4

This is a tasty way to stretch leftover roast chicken or turkey. In fact, roast beef or pork will do just as well.

Dressing:

2 tbsp	honey	25 mL
1 tbsp	Worcestershire sauce	15 mL
1 1/2 cups	SPICY SESAME VINAIGRETTE (see recipe, page 34)	375 mL

Salad:

2 cups	bean sprouts (preferably mung bean)	500 mL
2 tbsp	vegetable oil	25 mL
3	cloves garlic, peeled and very thinly sliced lengthwise	3
1 lb	Chinese-style steamed noodles or 8 oz (250 g) dried fettuccine	500 g
1 cup	English cucumber cut into thin matchsticks	250 mL
1 cup	carrots, cut into thin matchsticks	250 mL
2 cups	cooked chicken, beef or pork cut into julienne strips	500 mL
1/2 cup	thinly sliced green onions, green parts only	125 mL
2 tbsp	sesame seeds	25 mL

1. In a small bowl or pot, combine all dressing ingredients and mix well. (If necessary, warm dressing over low heat or in microwave to ensure honey is dissolved.)

2. In a large bowl of ice water, refresh bean sprouts for 15 minutes until crisp. Drain and set aside.

3. In a small skillet, heat oil over medium heat for 30 seconds. Add garlic and fry until golden, about 2 minutes. (Be careful not to let it burn.) With a slotted spoon, transfer garlic to a paper towel. Reserve oil.

4. In a large pot of boiling salted water, blanch noodles for 1 minute. Drain and, using chopsticks or two forks, toss to dry. (If using pasta, prepare according to package directions.) Transfer to large salad bowl, toss with reserved garlic oil and allow to cool.

5. Add bean sprouts, cucumber, carrots, chicken and green onions. Pour dressing evenly over salad; toss well. Sprinkle with sesame seeds and serve immediately.

SHRIMP AND CUCUMBER SUNOMONO SALAD

SERVES 4

AS AN APPETIZER

For this recipe, we've soaked the bean thread noodles longer than usual, as there's no further cooking.

2 oz	bean thread noodles	50 g
1/2	English cucumber, peeled	1/2
2 cups	water	500 mL
1 tbsp	salt	15 mL
6 oz	cooked, peeled shrimp	175 g
1 tbsp	toasted sesame seeds	15 mL
1 cup	GINGER SUNOMONO DRESSING (see recipe, page 35)	250 mL

1. In a heatproof bowl or pot, cover noodles with boiling water and soak for 5 minutes. Drain and chill.

2. On a cutting board, slice cucumber in half lengthwise. Cut into paper-thin slices.

3. In a mixing bowl, combine water and salt. Add cucumber slices and soak for 15 minutes. Drain, pat dry with paper towels and chill.

4. Just before serving, divide noodles into 4 bowls. Cover noodles with cucumber and top with shrimp. Pour 1/4 cup (50 mL) dressing over each salad and garnish with sesame seeds. Serve immediately.

RICE NOODLE SALAD WITH SUGAR SNAP PEAS, SWEET PEPPERS AND ALMONDS WITH NUOC CHAM

SERVES 4

To toast almonds, heat a dry heavy skillet over medium heat for 30 seconds. Add almonds and cook until they begin to turn golden, about 2 minutes. Immediately remove from heat, as they'll continue cooking until they cool.

8 oz	medium vermicelli (rice stick noodles) *or* dried fettuccine	250 g
2/3 cup	NUOC CHAM (see recipe, page 33)	150 mL
1 tbsp	butter	15 mL
1 tbsp	olive oil	15 mL
3 cups	trimmed sugar snap or snow peas	750 mL
2 tsp	minced garlic	10 mL
2 tbsp	vegetable or chicken stock	25 mL
1 cup	thinly sliced red bell peppers	250 mL
1 cup	thinly sliced yellow bell peppers	250 mL
1/2 cup	toasted sliced almonds	125 mL
1/4 cup	cilantro leaves	50 mL
	Coarsely ground black pepper, to taste	

1. In a heatproof bowl or pot, cover noodles with boiling water and soak for 5 minutes. (If using pasta, prepare according to package directions.) Drain, toss with 1/3 cup (75 mL) of the NUOC CHAM and let cool to room temperature.

2. In a nonstick pan, heat butter and oil over medium-high heat until just smoking. Add peas and stir-fry until well-coated, about 30 seconds. Add garlic and stock. Cover and cook until peas are tender-crisp, about 1 minute. Add peppers and stir-fry until warmed through and liquid is absorbed, about 1 minute. Remove from heat. Add remaining NUOC CHAM and mix well.

3. In a large salad bowl, combine noodles, vegetables, almonds and cilantro; toss. Sprinkle with black pepper to taste and serve.

VERMICELLI RICE NOODLE AND 5-SPICE MAPLE-CURED SALMON SALAD WITH A CHILI-PLUM VINAIGRETTE

SERVES 8

8 oz	5-SPICE MAPLE-CURED SALMON (see recipe, page 92) *or* lox *or* smoked salmon	250 g
8 oz	thin vermicelli (thin rice stick noodles)	250 g

<u>Vinaigrette:</u>

1/4 cup	plum sauce	50 mL
1/4 cup	rice vinegar	50 mL
1 tbsp	minced ginger root	15 mL
1 tbsp	prepared mustard, such as Dijon	15 mL
1 tsp	chili paste	5 mL
2 tbsp	water	25 mL
1/2 cup	vegetable oil, plus oil for tossing noodles	125 mL
2 cups	shredded romaine or iceberg lettuce	500 mL
1 cup	bean sprouts	250 mL
2 tbsp	toasted sesame seeds	25 mL

1. Cut salmon into thin slices (if required). Stack 3 or 4 slices and roll up tightly. With a sharp knife, cut roll into thin shreds. Repeat with remaining salmon.

2. In a heatproof bowl or pot, cover noodles with boiling water and soak for 5 minutes. Drain, toss with a little oil and set aside.

3. In a mixing bowl, combine plum sauce, rice vinegar, ginger root, mustard, chili paste and water; mix well. Using a whisk, stir continuously while adding the oil in a steady stream. Set aside.

4. Place noodles in a large serving bowl. Add salmon, lettuce, bean sprouts and dressing; mix well. Garnish with toasted sesame seeds and serve.

$\mathcal{F}$ISH

PEPPERED SALMON WITH STEAMED EGG NOODLES   88

PAN-ROASTED SNAPPER WITH GINGER AND SCALLION LO MEIN   90

HERB-CRUSTED SEA BASS WITH CHINESE RATATOUILLE RAMEN NOODLES   91

5-SPICE MAPLE CURED SALMON   92

UDON NOODLES WITH SPICY TOMATO, ANCHOVY, BASIL AND GARLIC SAUCE   93

BROAD EGG NOODLES WITH A SMOKED SALMON, ASPARAGUS, LEMON AND GINGER CREAM   94

BROAD EGG NOODLES WITH SALMON, RED PEPPER, ORANGE AND GINGER CREAM   95

SOY-BRAISED SNAPPER AND SHIITAKE MUSHROOMS WITH RICE STICK NOODLES   96

WUNTON NOODLES TOSSED WITH SHREDDED HALIBUT, LETTUCE AND A
SPICED CARROT JUICE BROTH   98

Peppered Salmon with Steamed Egg Noodles

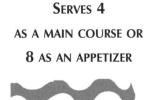

Serves 4

as a main course or

8 as an appetizer

Steamer, preferably bamboo

1 tsp	whole Szechwan peppercorns	5 mL
1 tsp	black peppercorns	5 mL
1 tbsp	oyster sauce	15 mL
2 tsp	soya sauce	10 mL
1 tsp	dark soya sauce *or* mushroom soya sauce	5 mL
2 tbsp	chicken stock *or* water	25 mL
1 tsp	cornstarch	5 mL
1 lb	Chinese style steamed noodles *or* 8 oz (250 g) dried spaghetti	500 g
2 tbsp	chicken stock	25 mL
2 tsp	sesame oil	10 mL
1 cup	bean sprouts	250 mL
2	green onions, green part only, sliced diagonally	2
2 tbsp	vegetable oil	25 mL
12 oz	boneless salmon fillet, cut into 1/2-inch (1 cm) square pieces	375 g
1	clove garlic, minced	1
2	shallots, thinly sliced	2
1 tbsp	dry sherry	15 mL
	Juice of half lemon (optional)	

1. In a dry frying pan, toast Szechwan and black peppercorns over medium heat until fragrant. Coarsely grind in a pepper grinder or mortar and pestle, or by crushing with a wine bottle between two sheets of wax paper. Set aside.

2. In a small bowl, combine oyster sauce, soya sauces, stock and cornstarch; mix well. Set aside.

3. In a bowl, cover noodles with hot water and separate strands by pulling them apart with your hands. (If using pasta, prepare according to package instructions.) Drain. In a heatproof bowl, combine noodles with stock, sesame oil, bean sprouts and green onions. Mix well. Place noodle mixture in a dish or shallow bowl and place in a steamer. Steam over medium heat for 4 minutes, or cover and microwave for 4 minutes. Keep warm.

4. In a nonstick wok or skillet, heat oil over medium-high heat for 30 seconds. Add salmon and sauté until golden, about 45 seconds on each side. Add peppercorns, garlic and shallots. Mix and cook for 30 seconds. Splash with sherry and toss for 15 seconds. Add sauce, stir gently and cook until sauce is thickened and salmon is well-coated, about 1 minute. Spoon salmon onto warm noodles. Add lemon juice and serve immediately.

PAN-ROASTED SNAPPER WITH GINGER AND SCALLION LO MEIN

SERVES 4

The pan-roasting method described here is a great way to keep the fish moist and succulent.

CHINESE RATATOUILLE RAMEN NOODLES (recipe, page 168) also works well as an alternative to GINGER AND SCALLION LO MEIN in this recipe.

Preheat oven to 400° F (200° F)
Ovenproof skillet or 9- by 13-inch (3 L) baking dish

1 lb	snapper or any firm white fish fillets	500 g
1 tsp	salt	5 mL
1 tsp	pepper	5 mL
2 tbsp	cornstarch	25 mL
1	recipe GINGER AND SCALLION LO MEIN (see recipe, page 170)	1
1 tbsp	vegetable oil	15 mL
2 tbsp	SPICY SESAME VINAIGRETTE (see recipe, page 34)	25 mL

1. In a mixing bowl, combine salt, pepper and cornstarch. Dredge fish in mixture until evenly coated.

2. Prepare GINGER AND SCALLION LO MEIN and keep warm.

3. In a large ovenproof skillet, heat oil over medium-high heat for 30 seconds. Add fish and fry until just golden, about 1 minute on each side. Transfer skillet to oven (or place fish in a baking dish, if using) and bake until fish flakes easily, about 5 minutes.

4. Brush fish with SPICY SESAME VINAIGRETTE. Arrange attractively on top of GINGER AND SCALLION LO MEIN and serve immediately.

HERB-CRUSTED SEA BASS WITH CHINESE RATATOUILLE RAMEN NOODLES

SERVES 4

If you can't find sea bass, use halibut, snapper or cod. If you feel like splurging, try mixing the herb mixture with 2 tbsp (25 mL) melted butter and spreading it on two split lobsters. Cook them under the broiler for about 5 minutes and serve with the CHINESE RATATOUILLE RAMEN NOODLES.

Preheat oven to 400° F (200° F)
Ovenproof skillet or 9- by 13-inch (3 L) baking dish

1	recipe CHINESE RATATOUILLE RAMEN NOODLES (see recipe, page 168)	1
1 lb	sea bass or any firm white fish fillets,cut into 4 pieces	500 g
1/2 tsp	salt	2 mL
1/2 tsp	pepper	2 mL
1 tbsp	minced fresh thyme	15 mL
1 tbsp	minced fresh oregano	15 mL
1 tbsp	minced fresh rosemary	15 mL
1 tbsp	vegetable oil	15 mL
1/2	lemon	1/2

1. Prepare CHINESE RATATOUILLE RAMEN NOODLES. Place on a serving platter and keep warm.

2. In a small bowl, combine thyme, oregano and rosemary. Season fish with salt and pepper. Rub herbs evenly onto one side of each piece until well coated.

3. In a large ovenproof skillet, heat oil over medium-high heat for 30 seconds. Add fish and fry, herb side down, until just golden, about 1 minute. Turn and repeat. Place skillet in oven with fish herb side up (or transfer fish to baking dish, if using) and bake until fish flakes easily, about 6 minutes. Arrange fish on CHINESE RATATOUILLE RAMEN NOODLES. Squeeze the juice of half lemon on fish and serve immediately.

5-SPICE MAPLE CURED SALMON

MAKES ABOUT 2 LBS (1 KG)

Vary the amount of salt for the size of the salmon. A large side (3-4 lbs [1.5 kg]) will use twice this mixture. Make sure to leave the skin on as it lessens salt penetration and makes the salmon easier to cut and handle.

This recipe provides a delicious and economical alternative to expensive smoked salmon.

1	side of salmon (about 2 lbs [1 kg])	1
1/2 cup	salt, preferably sea salt	125 mL
1/2 cup	maple syrup	125 mL
2 tbsp	soya sauce	25 mL
1 tbsp	grated ginger root	15 mL
1 tsp	HOME-STYLE 5-SPICE MIX (see recipe, page 28) *or* commercially prepared 5-spice powder	5 mL

1. Prepare the salmon by removing all bones and trimming sides of fat. Place the salmon in a long stainless steel, glass or plastic container.

2. In a small bowl combine salt, maple syrup, soya sauce, ginger root and 5-spice powder. Pour mixture over fish, turning to coat evenly. Leave salmon, skin-side down, cover with plastic wrap and place a weighted pan (or a couple of bricks) on top. Refrigerate at least 12 hours.

3. Remove salmon from curing mixture, and rinse off excess salt. Lay skin-side down on a cutting board and slice on a diagonal into thin slices without cutting through the skin. Leave skin behind.

UDON NOODLES WITH SPICY TOMATO, ANCHOVY, BASIL AND GARLIC SAUCE

SERVES 4

A great contribution to fast food, udon noodles are often sold pre-cooked in vacuum packages. Simply heat and serve. Udon looks like a fat spaghetti strand and ziti or spaghetti can be easily substituted. Since the large strands can be awkward, you might cut the noodles into manageable chunks before soaking.

1 lb	fresh udon noodles or ziti or spaghetti	500 g
1 tbsp	olive oil, plus oil for coating noodles	15 mL
1 tbsp	minced garlic	15 mL
2	tomatoes, finely diced	2
2 tbsp	chopped fresh basil (or 1/2 tsp [2 mL] dried)	25 mL
5	anchovy fillets, finely chopped	5
	Hot pepper sauce, to taste	
4 tbsp	grated Parmesan cheese	60 mL

1. In a heatproof bowl or pot, cover noodles with boiling water and soak for 3 minutes. (If using pasta, prepare according to package directions.) Drain, toss with a little oil and set aside.

2. In a nonstick wok or skillet, heat oil over medium-high heat for 30 seconds. Add garlic and cook until it begins to sizzle and change color. Add tomatoes, stir and heat through. Add basil, anchovies and hot sauce and cook for 1 minute. Add noodles and toss until heated through. Stir in the cheese and serve immediately.

BROAD EGG NOODLES WITH A SMOKED SALMON, ASPARAGUS, LEMON AND GINGER CREAM

SERVES 6

Smoked salmon, asparagus and lemon are a classic combination.

Fresh or dried fettuccine (of any flavor) can be used with great results.

Remove rind from lemon with a zester or potato peeler before cutting and squeezing out the juice.

12 oz	dried broad egg noodles, *or* fettuccine	375 g
	Vegetable oil for coating noodles	
	Juice of 1 lemon	
1 tbsp	lemon zest	15 mL
1 tsp	minced ginger root	5 mL
1 tsp	honey	5 mL
1 cup	whipping (35%) cream	250 mL
1 cup	sparkling apple cider	250 mL
1 lb	asparagus, woody ends discarded, peeled and cut into 1-inch (2.5 cm) pieces	500 g
1 tbsp	cornstarch dissolved in 2 tbsp (25 mL)water	15 mL
4 oz	smoked salmon *or* 5-SPICE MAPLE-CURED SALMON (see recipe, page 92), coarsely chopped	125 g
	Salt and pepper to taste	

1. In a large pot of boiling salted water, cook noodles until *al dente*, about 5 or 6 minutes. (If using pasta, prepare according to package directions.) Drain, toss with a little oil and set aside.

2. In a nonstick wok or skillet, combine lemon juice and zest, ginger root, honey, whipping cream and apple cider; bring to a boil. Reduce heat to medium. Add asparagus and simmer until tender, about 5 to 8 minutes. Add dissolved cornstarch and stir until mixture thickens. Add salmon and season with salt and pepper. Add noodles and toss well. Serve immediately.

Broad Egg Noodles with Salmon, Red Pepper, Orange and Ginger Cream

Serves 4

Salmon is an amazing fish — flavorful, healthy and used in many different cuisines. Here it's part of a sophisticated noodle dish.

Toss in the salmon just before serving to preserve its silky texture and avoid overcooking.

1 lb	fresh broad egg noodles *or* fresh fettuccine	500 g
	Vegetable oil for coating noodles	
1 cup	whipping (35%) cream	250 mL
1 cup	white wine	250 mL
1 tbsp	minced ginger root	15 mL
	Juice of 1 orange	1
1 tbsp	orange zest	15 mL
8 oz	salmon, cut into 1/2-inch (1 cm) cubes	250 g
2	red peppers, seeded and sliced	2
2 cups	washed, chopped Chinese mustard greens *or* spinach, packed down	500 mL
1 tbsp	cornstarch dissolved in 2 tbsp (25 mL) water	15 mL
	Salt and pepper to taste	

1. In a large pot of boiling salted water, cook noodles until *al dente*, about 5 or 6 minutes. (If using pasta, prepare according to the package instructions.) Drain, toss with a little vegetable oil and set aside.

2. In a nonstick wok or skillet combine cream, wine, ginger root, orange juice and zest. Bring to a boil. Reduce heat to medium. Add peppers and simmer until soft, about 5 to 8 minutes.

3. Add salmon to pan and season with salt and pepper. Add dissolved cornstarch and stir until sauce thickens. Reduce heat to low and simmer for 3 to 4 minutes. Add spinach and noodles, toss well and serve immediately.

SOY-BRAISED SNAPPER AND SHIITAKE MUSHROOMS WITH RICE STICK NOODLES

SERVES 4

This dish combines the earthy texture of fresh shiitake mushrooms in a deep, rich broth. Any firm white-fleshed fish can be used — we often use black cod.

Make this one-pot meal in a casserole dish or for a rustic touch, an inexpensive Chinese sand pot. This very porous type of pottery is often lined with a ceramic glaze. It must be soaked in water before use or it will crack when exposed to heat. It is also very fragile and won't stand up to rough use.

Preheat oven to 350° F (180° F)
9- by 13-inch (3 L) baking dish or Chinese sand pot

1 tbsp	vegetable oil	15 mL
1	onion, coarsely chopped	1
1 tsp	minced garlic	5 mL
1 tsp	minced ginger root	5 mL
12	fresh shiitake mushrooms *or* button mushrooms, sliced	12
1	red pepper, seeded and diced	1
1	carrot, peeled and thinly sliced	1
4 cups	chicken or fish stock	1 L
2 tbsp	dark soya sauce	25 mL
1 tbsp	cornstarch dissolved in 2 tbsp (25 mL) water	15 mL
1 lb	fresh snapper fillets, or any firm white fish, cut into 1-inch (2.5 cm) cubes	500 g
4 oz	thin vermicelli (thin rice stick noodles) *or* angel hair pasta	125 g
	Black pepper to taste	
1/4 cup	sliced green onions for garnish	50 mL

1. In a large heavy-bottomed saucepan, heat oil over medium-high heat for 30 seconds. Add onion and sauté until it softens and begins to change color. Add garlic and ginger root, sauté for 1 minute. Add mushrooms, red pepper and carrot; mix well.

2. Add stock and soya sauce and bring mixture to a simmer. Add dissolved cornstarch and stir until the mixture begins to thicken. Transfer to a baking dish, if using.

RICE NOODLES WITH BEEF, GREEN BEANS AND TOMATOES (PAGE 122) ➤

OVERLEAF: PEPPERED SALMON WITH STEAMED EGG NOODLES (PAGE 88) ➤

3. Lightly crush noodles in the package so they break into little pieces. Place in a colander and rinse with boiling water. (If using pasta, prepare according to package directions.)

4. Add noodles and fish to sauce and stir well. Cover with lid, or a piece of tinfoil, and bake for 15 minutes. Serve immediately, garnished with green onions.

◅ Lemon Grass Pork Chops with Chinese Pesto Noodles (page 132)

WUNTON NOODLES TOSSED WITH SHREDDED HALIBUT, LETTUCE AND A SPICED CARROT JUICE BROTH

SERVES 4

The lightly cooked halibut is the key to this delicious dish. It features an interesting texture and an unusual spicy-sweet taste.

1 lb	fresh wunton noodles *or* 8 oz (250 g) dried angel hair pasta	500 g
	Vegetable oil for coating noodles	
2 cups	carrot juice	500 mL
2 tbsp	rice vinegar	25 mL
1 tbsp	minced ginger root	15 mL
3	kaffir lime leaves *or* 1 tsp (5 mL) lime zest	3
1 tsp	chili paste	5 mL
1 tbsp	cornstarch, dissolved in 2 tbsp (25 mL) water	15 mL
4 oz	halibut, cut into thin slices, each cut into 1/4-inch (5 mm) pieces	125 g
2 cups	shredded lettuce	500 mL
	Salt and pepper	

1. In a large pot of boiling salted water, cook noodles until *al dente*, about 1 or 2 minutes. (If using pasta, prepare according to package instructions.) Drain, toss with a little oil and set aside.

2. In a nonstick wok or skillet, combine carrot juice, vinegar, ginger root, lime leaves and chili paste; bring almost to a boil. Quickly add dissolved cornstarch. Stir to thicken, then reduce heat. (Don't boil the sauce or the carrot juice will separate; if this happens, pulse the mixture in a blender until smooth.)

3. Add halibut and lettuce to carrot juice mixture and season with salt and pepper. Cook gently for 1 to 2 minutes, stirring occasionally.

4. Add noodles to the pan; toss well to mix. Heat to warm through, about 1 or 2 minutes. Season with salt and pepper and serve immediately.

SEAFOOD

MOO SHU-STYLE PRAWNS WITH SPINACH NOODLES

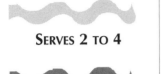

SERVES 2 TO 4

Moo Shu pork is a famous dish from Northern China. It usually calls for "cloud ear mushrooms" and "dried lilybuds" and is accompanied by crepe-like pancakes. This adaptation uses more readily available ingredients.

For an interesting variation, try using tomato-herb fettuccine.

8	dried Chinese mushrooms or other type of dried mushrooms	8
1 lb	fresh spinach noodles *or* fettuccine	500 g
2 tbsp	vegetable oil, plus oil for coating noodles	25 mL
2 tbsp	dry sherry	25 mL
1 tbsp	hoisin sauce	15 mL
1 tbsp	fish sauce	15 mL
1 tbsp	dark soya sauce	15 mL
2	large eggs, beaten	2
1 tbsp	minced garlic	15 mL
1 tbsp	finely chopped ginger root	15 mL
4	slices back bacon, cut into thin strips	4
1/4 cup	chicken stock	50 mL
24	tiger prawns or large shrimp, shelled and deveined	24
1 cup	yellow Chinese chives, cut into matchsticks, *or* thinly sliced green onions	250 mL
1 cup	fresh enoki mushrooms, *or* canned bamboo shoots, cut into matchsticks	250 mL
	Salt and pepper to taste	

1. In a heatproof bowl or pot, soak mushrooms in 2 cups (500 mL) boiling water for 15 minutes. Strain and reserve liquid. Discard stems and slice caps thinly. Set aside.

2. In a large pot of boiling salted water, cook noodles until *al dente*. (If using pasta, prepare according to package directions.) Drain, toss with a little oil and set aside.

3. In a small bowl, combine sherry, hoisin sauce, fish sauce, soya sauce and 2 tbsp (25 mL) of the reserved mushroom liquid. Set aside.

4. In a nonstick wok or skillet, heat 1 tbsp (15 mL) oil over medium heat for 30 seconds. Add eggs, tilting pan while cooking so liquid runs to the edge and the omelet is very thin. Flip and cook briefly. Transfer omelet to a plate and allow to cool. Cut omelet into thin strips 2 inches (5 cm) long. Set aside.

5. In the same pan, heat remaining oil over high heat until it is just beginning to smoke. Add mushrooms, garlic, ginger root and bacon; stir-fry for 1 minute. Add chicken stock and bring to a boil. Add prawns and cook until they turn pink and opaque. Add sherry mixture and stir briefly to mix. Add noodles, mix well and cook until heated through and liquid is absorbed, about 2 minutes. Add egg strips, chives and enoki mushrooms; toss and cook until heated through, about 1 minute. Season to taste and serve immediately.

SILVER NEEDLES WITH PANCETTA AND SHRIMP

SERVES 2 TO 4

Silver needles are fresh, ready-to-use rice noodles resembling elongated spaetzles with pointy ends. If you can't find them in your local Asian markets, use flat rice stick noodles, or penne pasta.

1 tbsp	vegetable oil	15 mL
2	eggs, beaten	2
4 oz	pancetta *or* back bacon, cut in thin strips	125 g
2 tsp	finely chopped garlic	10 mL
4 oz	large shrimp, peeled and deveined	125 g
1/2 cup	thinly sliced red bell peppers	125 mL
1/2 cup	chopped green onions *or* Chinese chives	125 mL
1/4 cup	chicken stock	50 mL
2 tbsp	fish sauce	25 mL
8 oz	silver needle noodles *or* broad rice vermicelli (broad rice stick noodles) *or* penne pasta	250 g
	Vegetable oil for coating vermicelli or pasta, if using	
1 cup	bean sprouts	250 mL
1 tsp	Japanese 7-spice *or* coarsely ground pepper	5 mL
2 tbsp	grated Parmesan cheese	25 mL

1. If using silver needles, place in a colander and rinse with hot water; set aside. If using dried noodles, soak in a heatproof bowl or pot in boiling water for 5 minutes. (If using pasta, prepare according to package instructions.) Drain. Coat with a little oil, if necessary; set aside.

2. In a nonstick wok or skillet, heat 1 tbsp (15 mL) oil over medium heat for 30 seconds. Add eggs, tilting pan while cooking so liquid runs to the edge and the omelet is very thin. Flip and cook briefly. Transfer omelet to a plate and allow to cool. Cut omelet into thin strips 2 inches (5 cm) long. Set aside.

3. In same skillet, over medium heat, sauté pancetta for 2 minutes or until just crisp. Drain any excess fat. Add garlic and shrimp and sauté for 1 minute or until shrimp just turns opaque. Add peppers, green onions, stock and fish sauce; stir and bring to boil. Add noodles and stir-fry for 2 minutes or until liquid is absorbed.

4. Remove pan from heat. Add bean sprouts and omelet strips, season with 7-spice or pepper and salt; mix well. Transfer to serving platter, sprinkle with Parmesan and serve immediately.

Cellophane-Fried Shrimp in Spicy Tomato Coulis

SERVES 4

2	tomatoes, peeled, seeded and coarsely chopped	2
2 tbsp	bottled clam juice	25 mL
1-2 tsp	*sambal* (Vietnamese chili sauce) *or* dried chili flakes	5-10 mL
1 tbsp	pernod or anisette (optional)	15 mL
2 tbsp	chopped cilantro	25 mL
	Sugar to taste	
	Salt to taste	
24	tiger prawns or large shrimp	24
2 tbsp	*mirin* or 2 tbsp (25 mL) honey, mixed with 2 tbsp (25 mL) sherry	25 mL
1/2 tsp	salt	2 mL
2 tsp	minced ginger root	10 mL
1 tbsp	soya sauce	15 mL
2 oz	bean thread noodles	50 g
4 cups	vegetable oil for deep-frying	1 L
1/4 cup	cornstarch	50 mL
2	egg whites, beaten just until foamy	2

1. Put tomatoes, clam juice, sambal, pernod (if using) and cilantro in food processor or blender; puree until liquefied. Season with sugar and salt. Adjust spiciness by adding more chili sauce, if desired. Set aside in refrigerator.

2. Peel shrimp, leaving tail segment of shell attached. Butterfly each shrimp by scoring its underside lengthwise with a sharp knife, exposing the vein. Be careful not to cut shrimp in half; remove and discard vein.

3. In a bowl combine *mirin*, salt, ginger root and soya sauce; add shrimp and toss to coat. Set aside for 20 minutes.

4. Inside a plastic bag, cut noodles into small pieces with a sharp pair of scissors. If scissors don't work, cut with a heavy knife or cleaver. Transfer to a medium-size bowl and set aside.

5. In a wok, saucepan or deep fryer, heat oil to 275° F (140° C), or until a piece of noodle dropped in oil sizzles and immediately puffs up.

6. In another plastic bag, toss shrimp with cornstarch until evenly coated. Dip each shrimp in egg white and dredge through noodle bits to coat well. Fry in hot oil, 3 or 4 at a time, until golden and crisp. With a slotted spoon, transfer cooked shrimp to paper towel; keep warm until all are cooked. Serve immediately, accompanied by tomato coulis as dipping sauce.

EGG NOODLES WITH CRAB AND ASPARAGUS

SERVES 4

Fresh, sweet crab meat and crunchy, just-picked asparagus is a combination made in heaven.

If you don't have access to fresh crab, use canned, or substitute fresh cooked shrimp.

When fiddleheads are in season, they make an interesting alternative to asparagus. Make sure they're trimmed and thoroughly washed before using.

1 lb	fresh thin egg noodles or 8 oz (250 g) dried	500 g
2 tsp	sesame oil	10 mL
Pinch	salt and pepper	Pinch
1 tbsp	olive oil	15 mL
1 tsp	minced garlic	5 mL
2 tsp	minced ginger root	10 mL
8 oz	asparagus, peeled and cut diagonally into 1/2-inch (1 cm) lengths *or* snow peas	250 g
1/4 cup	white wine	50 mL
1 tbsp	fish sauce	15 mL
8 oz	cooked fresh crab meat *or* 2 cans (4.2 oz [130 g]) chunk crabmeat *or* 8 oz (250 g) cooked shrimp	250 g
1/4 cup	chopped fresh herbs (parsley, thyme, basil, etc.)	125 mL
	Grated Parmesan cheese (optional)	

1. In a large pot of boiling salted water, cook noodles until *al dente*, about 3 minutes. (If using dried noodles, prepare according to package directions.) Drain. Toss with sesame oil and sprinkle with salt and pepper. Set aside in large bowl and keep warm.

2. In a nonstick wok or skillet, heat oil over medium-high heat for 30 seconds. Add garlic, ginger root and asparagus and stir until well coated. Add wine and fish sauce and bring to a boil for 1 minute or until asparagus is tender-crisp. Add crab and cook until warm through. Remove from heat. Add herbs and toss to mix.

3. Pour crab mixture over noodles and toss to mix. Sprinkle with Parmesan, if desired, and serve immediately.

STIR-FRIED CHOW MEIN NOODLES WITH A CLAM, ORANGE JUICE AND BLACK BEAN SAUCE

SERVES 4

If your tastebuds are in the doldrums, try this. The orange juice and black bean sauce combine to create a spicy and tangy base for the clams and crispy noodles.

1 lb	fresh chow mein noodles	500 g
1 tbsp	vegetable oil, plus oil for coating noodles	15 mL
1	red onion, peeled and sliced	1
1	red or green pepper, seeded and thinly sliced	1
1 tsp	minced ginger root	5 mL
1 tbsp	minced garlic	25 mL
1 1/2 cups	orange juice	375 mL
2 tbsp	black bean sauce	25 mL
1 tbsp	cornstarch dissolved in 2 tbsp (25 mL) water	15 mL
	Hot pepper sauce to taste	
1	can 14 oz (400 mL) clam meat *or* 2 lbs (1 kg) fresh clams	1

1. In a heatproof bowl or pot, cover noodles with boiling water and soak for 5 minutes. Drain, toss with a little oil and set aside.

2. In a small saucepan, combine onion, pepper, ginger root, garlic, orange juice and black bean sauce. Bring to a boil. Add dissolved cornstarch and stir until sauce begins to thicken. Add hot pepper sauce, to taste. Add clam meat, stir and heat through. Set aside. (If using fresh clams, heat for 4 to 5 minutes, until they open.)

3. In a nonstick wok or skillet, heat oil over medium-high heat for 30 seconds. Add noodles and stir-fry until they begin to crisp, about 5 minutes. Add sauce and toss to coat the noodles evenly. (If using fresh clams, transfer noodles to a platter, then cover with sauce.) Serve immediately.

RICE VERMICELLI IN COCONUT CURRY WITH SEAFOOD

SERVES 4

This is a richer and more complex version of the Chinese noodle shop classic.

8 oz	thin rice vermicelli (thin rice stick noodles) *or* angel hair pasta	250 g
2 tbsp	vegetable oil, plus oil for coating noodles	25 mL
2	eggs, beaten	2
6 oz	small raw shrimp, shelled	175 g
4 oz	thinly sliced scallops	125 g
	Salt and pepper to taste	
1 cup	coconut milk	250 mL
1 tbsp	Madras curry powder	15 mL
2 tbsp	soya sauce	25 mL
3/4 cup	celery, sliced diagonally into 1-inch (2.5 cm) pieces	175 mL
2 cups	bean sprouts, packed down	500 mL
1/2 cup	thin diagonally sliced green onions	125 mL
2 tbsp	chopped cilantro	25 mL

1. In a heatproof bowl or pot, cover noodles with boiling water and soak for 3 minutes. (If using pasta, prepare according to package directions.) Drain, coat with a little oil and set aside.

2. In a nonstick wok or skillet, heat 1 tbsp (15 mL) of the oil over medium-high heat for 30 seconds. Add eggs and tilt the pan while cooking so liquid runs to the edge and the omelet is very thin. Flip and cook briefly. Transfer omelet to a plate and allow to cool. Cut omelet into thin strips 2 inches (5 cm) long. Set aside.

3. In the same pan, heat remaining oil over high heat for 30 seconds. Add shrimp and stir-fry for 1 minute. Add scallops and stir-fry for 30 seconds. Season to taste with salt and pepper. Remove with a slotted spoon and keep warm.

4. In the same pan, heat coconut milk and curry powder over medium-high heat until boiling. Add noodles and soya sauce; mix well. Cook until liquid is mostly absorbed, about 3 minutes. Add seafood mixture, omelet strips, celery, bean sprouts and green onions; stir to mix well. Cook for 1 minute, then transfer to a serving dish. Garnish with cilantro and serve immediately.

STIR-FRIED SCALLOPS AND ASPARAGUS IN A GARLIC, SOYA AND BLACK PEPPER SAUCE OVER A CRISPY NOODLE CAKE

SERVES 4

AS A MAIN COURSE OR

6 AS AN APPETIZER

Influenced by Cantonese cooking, this also works well as an appetizer — just cut the noodles into small wedges and top with sauce.

The noodle cake can be made up to 1 hour in advance and warmed in the oven just before the sauce is cooked.

Preheat oven to 375° F (190° C)
Baking sheet

1 lb	fresh chow mein noodles	500 g
2 tbsp	sliced green onions	25 mL
2 tbsp	vegetable oil, plus oil for coating noodles	25 mL
1 tbsp	minced ginger root	15 mL
4 oz	fresh asparagus, woody ends discarded, cut into 1-inch (2.5 cm) pieces	125 g
4 oz	ocean scallops	125 g
1 tbsp	minced garlic	15 mL
1 tsp	sesame oil	5 mL
1 tbsp	soya sauce	15 mL
1 tbsp	cilantro	15 mL
1 tsp	coarsely ground black pepper	5 mL
1 cup	chicken or fish stock	250 mL
1 tbsp	cornstarch dissolved in 2 tbsp (25 mL) water	15 mL

1. In a heatproof bowl or pot, cover noodles with boiling water and soak for 5 minutes. Drain, coat with a little oil and toss with green onions.

2. In a nonstick wok or skillet, heat 1 tbsp (15 mL) of the oil over medium-high heat for 30 seconds. Add noodles and stir-fry until coated in oil. Cook over medium heat, shaking the pan occasionally, for 10 minutes or until bottom is golden brown. Press down to make a compact pancake. Flip noodle pancake over, and continue cooking for another 10 minutes, or until the bottom is golden brown. Transfer to a baking sheet and keep warm in oven.

3. In a nonstick wok or skillet, heat remaining oil over high heat for 30 seconds. Sauté ginger root until it starts to sizzle. Add asparagus and sauté for 3 to 4 minutes. Add scallops and garlic and stir-fry until scallops are firm and the garlic is fragrant, but not browned. Add sesame oil, soya sauce, cilantro, black pepper and stock. Bring to a boil, add dissolved cornstarch and stir constantly until thickened. To serve, place noodle cake (or individual wedges) on a serving plate and cover with sauce.

RICE STICK NOODLES WITH CRAB IN A BASIL-TOMATO SAUCE

SERVES 4

In this simple but delicious dish, thin rice stick noodles are combined with a distinctly West Coast combination of crab, tomatoes and basil. Although best with fresh crab, a can of snow crab, lightly rinsed in water to reduce the salt, will do just fine.

8 oz	thin vermicelli (thin rice stick noodles) *or* spaghettini	250 g
4 oz	fresh or canned crab meat	125 g
1	can (19 oz [398 mL]) tomatoes, including juice	1
1	onion, diced	1
1 tsp	minced garlic	5 mL
2 tbsp	finely chopped basil (or 1/2 tsp [1 mL] dried)	25 mL
1 tbsp	extra virgin olive oil, plus oil for coating noodles	15 mL
	Salt and pepper to taste	

1. In a heatproof bowl or pot, cover noodles with boiling water and soak for 3 minutes. (If using pasta, prepare according to package instructions.) Drain, toss with a little olive oil and set aside.

2. In a medium-sized bowl, crush tomatoes with a fork (or process on and off in a food processor) until they are in bite-sized pieces.

3. In a nonstick wok or skillet, heat oil over medium-high heat for 30 seconds. Add onions and garlic and cook, stirring often, until onions have softened and are just beginning to color, about 5 minutes. Add tomatoes and their juice. Increase heat and cook until liquid is reduced and sauce is slightly thickened, about 5 minutes.

4. Reduce heat to a gentle simmer, add the crab, stir, and cook for 2 to 3 minutes. Add basil and noodles and mix well to distribute the sauce. Season with salt and pepper; serve immediately.

RICE NOODLES, SCALLOPS AND BROCCOLI IN A GARLIC, SOY AND BLACK PEPPER SAUCE

SERVES 4

If you're lucky enough to have access to fresh scallops in the shell, here's what to do: Allow 4 per person, cover the skillet when cooking and serve on top of the noodle mixture.

For an interesting variation, try replacing broccoli with an equal quantity of other green vegetables, such as spinach, mustard greens and kale.

1 tsp	vegetable oil	5 mL
1	onion, sliced	1
1 tbsp	minced garlic	15 mL
2 cups	small broccoli florets	500 mL
2 cups	chicken or fish stock	500 mL
2 tbsp	sweet soya sauce *or* SWEET SOYA SAUCE SUBSTITUTE (see recipe, page 36)	25 mL
8 oz	large sea scallops	250 g
1 tbsp	cornstarch (dissolved in 2 tbsp [25 mL] water)	15 mL
1 tsp	cracked black pepper	5 mL
	Salt to taste	
1 lb	fresh rice noodles *or* fettuccine	500 g

1. In a nonstick wok or skillet heat oil over medium-high heat for 30 seconds. Add onions and garlic and sauté, stirring often, until onions have softened and are beginning to brown, about 5 minutes. Add broccoli, stock and soya sauce. Return to a boil and simmer until broccoli is tender, about 3 to 4 minutes.

2. Add scallops to the mixture. Return to a boil and add dissolved cornstarch, stirring until sauce begins to thicken. Add pepper; season to taste with salt.

3. In a mixing bowl, cover noodles with warm water and separate them with your fingers. Drain. (If using pasta, prepare according to package directions.) Add noodles to scallop mixture and heat until soft and heated through, about 3 minutes. Serve immediately.

RICE STICK NOODLES WITH MIXED SEAFOOD IN A MISO, GARLIC AND TOMATO SAUCE

SERVES 4

We recommend using sweet miso *for this dish. If you can only find the saltier varieties of* miso *paste, then reduce the quantity to suit your taste.*

4 oz	thin rice stick noodles (thin vermicelli) *or* angel hair pasta	125 g
1 tbsp	vegetable oil, plus oil for coating the noodles	15 mL
1	onion, diced	1
1 tbsp	minced garlic	15 mL
2 cups	tomato juice	500 mL
2 tbsp	sweet *miso* paste	25 mL
1 tsp	sesame oil	5 mL
1 tsp	chili sauce *or* hot pepper sauce	5 mL
1 tbsp	minced cilantro	15 mL
4 oz	large shrimp, peeled and deveined	125 g
4 oz	sea scallops	125 g
4 oz	salmon, cut in 1/2-inch (1 cm) cubes	125 g

1. In a heatproof bowl or pot, cover noodles with boiling water and soak for 3 minutes. (If using pasta, prepare according to package directions.) Drain, coat with a little vegetable oil and set aside.

2. In a large heavy-bottomed saucepan, heat oil over medium-high heat for 30 seconds. Add onion and garlic and sauté until onion has softened and begins to color, about 3 to 4 minutes. Add tomato juice, *miso*, sesame oil and chili sauce. Bring to a boil; reduce heat and simmer 5 minutes.

3. Add cilantro, shrimp, scallops and salmon to tomato mixture. Heat until seafood is firm and just cooked, about 2 to 3 minutes. (The salmon will be medium rare.) Add noodles and heat through for 1 to 2 minutes. Serve immediately.

PAN-FRIED THIN WHEAT NOODLES WITH SHRIMP, SOYA, GARLIC AND CHILI

SERVES 4 TO 6

Here's a simple-but-sumptuous version of that old favorite, shrimp with noodles. In this recipe we add onion and chili, and we glaze the noodles with soya to provide an interesting texture. Try making it with soba noodles for a change.

Preheat oven to 375° F (190° C)

10-inch (25 cm) ovenproof frying pan (or cast iron skillet) or 13-by 9-inch (3 L) baking dish

1 lb	thin dried wheat noodles *or* linguine	500 g
1 tbsp	vegetable oil, plus oil for coating noodles	15 mL
1	onion, finely diced	1
1 tbsp	minced garlic	15 mL
1 tsp	chili sauce	5 mL
1 tbsp	chopped cilantro	15 mL
8 oz	large shrimp, peeled	250 g
2 tbsp	sweet soya sauce *or* SWEET SOYA SAUCE SUBSTITUTE (see recipe, page 36)	25 mL
	Salt and pepper to taste	

1. In a large pot of boiling salted water, cook the noodles until *al dente*, about 4 to 5 minutes. (If using pasta, prepare according to package instructions.) Drain, toss with a little oil and set aside.

2. In a nonstick wok or skillet, heat oil over medium-high heat for 30 seconds. Add onion and garlic; sauté until onion softens and begins to color, about 2 to 3 minutes. Add chili sauce, cilantro and shrimp. Sauté until shrimp begin to turn pink, about 1 to 2 minutes.

3. Add noodles to skillet and drizzle soya sauce over top. Stir the mixture until soya sauce is evenly distributed; season to taste with salt and pepper. Place skillet in oven (or transfer contents to a baking dish, if using) and roast for 5 minutes. Serve immediately.

SEAFOOD VEGETABLE BROCHETTES WITH WASABI-LIME BUTTER AND CHINESE NOODLE ROSTI

SERVES 4

AS A MAIN COURSE

8 AS AN APPETIZER

Wasabi, sometime called Japanese horseradish, has a sharp, spicy flavor and is typically served with sushi and sashimi. You can buy it in gourmet food shops or oriental markets in a paste or a powder, to which water is added.

Soaking the skewers prevents burning.

Preheat broiler or, if using, start barbecue
Baking sheet

1	recipe CHINESE NOODLE AND SCALLION ROSTI (see page 166)	1
8 oz	snapper or other firm flesh fish fillet, cut into 16 1-inch (2.5 cm) cubes	250 g
8	large shrimp or prawns, peeled and deveined	8
8	large scallops	8
1	large red bell pepper, seeded and cut into 16 1-inch (2.5 cm) cubes	1
1	zucchini, cut into 8 slices 1 inch (2.5 cm) thick	1
8	mushrooms	8
8	long wood or bamboo skewers, soaked in water for 4 hours	8

Wasabi-Lime Butter:

2 tbsp	saki or white wine	25 mL
2 tsp	wasabi paste or powder	10 mL
2 tbsp	fresh lime juice	25 mL
2 tbsp	dark soya sauce	25 mL
1 tbsp	fish sauce	15 mL
1 tbsp	honey	15 mL
1-2 tbsp	chilled butter	15-25 mL

1. Prepare CHINESE NOODLE AND SCALLION ROSTI. Keep warm.

2. Thread equal portions of vegetables and seafood onto skewers attractively, starting with zucchini and ending with a mushroom. Arrange brochettes on a baking sheet lined with aluminum foil and set aside. Place oven rack 6 inches (15 cm) from heat.

3. In a nonreactive (or nonstick) saucepan, combine all wasabi-lime butter ingredients, except butter. Bring to a boil and cook over high heat, stirring constantly, until wasabi and honey are dissolved, about 30 seconds. Reduce heat to low. Add butter and whisk until butter is melted. The sauce should be slightly thickened.

4. Using a brush, baste brochettes generously with sauce. Place brochettes under broiler (or on barbecue) and broil for 2 minutes. Turn, baste and broil for 2 minutes or until ingredients begin to turn golden brown. Serve immediately over warm noodle rosti.

SPICY SQUID WITH SHANGHAI NOODLES

SERVES 4 TO 6

Squid is inexpensive, tasty and easy to prepare. The secret is not to overcook it — otherwise it becomes quite chewy.

Cuttlefish, which are oval in shape and much larger than squid, can also be used in this recipe.

1 lb	fresh Shanghai noodles *or* 8 oz (250 g) thin dried wheat noodles *or* 8 oz (250 g) dried spaghetti	500 g
2 tbsp	vegetable oil, plus oil for coating noodles	25 mL
12 oz	squid, cleaned	375 g
1/4 cup	chicken stock	50 mL
2 tbsp	soya sauce	25 mL
1 tsp	sugar	5 mL
2 tsp	Chinese black vinegar *or* balsamic vinegar	10 mL
1 tsp	sesame oil	5 mL
1	small onion, sliced	1
1 tbsp	minced ginger root	15 mL
1 tbsp	minced garlic	15 mL
1/2 tsp	HOME-STYLE 5-SPICE MIX (see recipe, page 28) *or* commercially prepared 5-spice powder	2 mL
2 tsp	chili bean paste	10 mL
1 tbsp	dry sherry	15 mL
1	red chili pepper *or* jalapeno, seeded and finely chopped	1
1	medium green bell pepper, seeded and sliced	1
1	medium red or yellow bell pepper, seeded and sliced	1
	Salt and pepper to taste	

1. In a heatproof bowl or pot, cover fresh noodles with boiling water and soak for 5 minutes. (If using dried noodles or pasta, prepare according to package directions.) Drain, coat with a little oil and set aside.

2. Under cold water, rinse squid thoroughly. Using a sharp pair of kitchen shears, make a cut along one side of the body and open up to make one flat piece. With a sharp knife, score outside surface of body lightly, making diagonal cuts about 1/4 inch (5 mm) apart in a crisscross pattern. Be careful not to cut through the meat. Cut into 2-inch (5 cm) squares.

3. Make the sauce: In a small bowl, combine stock, soya sauce, sugar, vinegar and sesame oil; mix well. Set aside.

4. In a nonstick wok or skillet, heat 1 tbsp (15 mL) of the oil until just beginning to smoke. Add onion, ginger root, garlic, 5-spice powder and chili bean paste; stir-fry for 30 seconds. Add squid and stir-fry until it just turns opaque and begins to curl, about 45 seconds. Splash with sherry and cook for 15 seconds. Transfer squid mixture to a bowl. Set aside.

5. In same skillet, heat remaining 1 tbsp (15 mL) oil for 10 seconds. Add peppers and stir-fry for 30 seconds. Add sauce mixture and bring to a boil. Add noodles and stir-fry until noodles are warmed through and sauce is mostly absorbed, about 2 minutes. Season with salt and pepper to taste. Add squid mixture, stir to mix and serve immediately.

MEAT

RICE NOODLES WITH BEEF, GREEN BEANS AND TOMATOES

SERVES 4

If you can find yard-long beans (usually in Asian markets) try them in this recipe. They're very tender and require less cooking time than regular beans.

If you don't have hoisin sauce, try tomato ketchup, which will also add sweetness to the dish.

Marinade:

1 tbsp	soya sauce	15 mL
1 tbsp	dark soya sauce *or* mushroom soya sauce	15 mL
1/2 tsp	sugar	2 mL
2 tbsp	dry sherry	25 mL
1/2 tsp	freshly ground black pepper	2 mL
1 tbsp	cornstarch	15 mL
12 oz	sirloin steak, cut into thin strips	375 g
4 or 5	medium tomatoes	4 or 5
8 oz	green beans, trimmed and sliced diagonally into 2-inch (5 cm) pieces	250 g
1 lb	fresh flat rice noodles *or* 8 oz (250 g) broad vermicelli (broad rice stick noodles)	500 g
2 tbsp	vegetable oil, plus oil for coating noodles	25 mL
1	small onion, sliced	1
2 tsp	minced garlic	10 mL
2 tsp	minced ginger root	10 mL
1/2 cup	chicken stock	125 mL
1 tbsp	hoisin sauce	15 mL
	Salt and pepper to taste	

1. In a small bowl, combine ingredients for marinade and mix well. Add beef and set aside to marinate for 20 minutes or overnight in refrigerator.

2. Blanch tomatoes in boiling water for 30 seconds. Over a bowl, peel, core and seed them. Chop tomatoes into 2-inch (5 cm) cubes. Strain any accumulated juices from bowl and reserve. Place tomato chunks in a sieve over bowl. Sprinkle lightly with salt and set aside to drain.

3. In a pot of boiling salted water, cook beans until tender-crisp, about 4 minutes. Drain and set aside.

4. In a colander, break up fresh rice noodles by running hot water over them and separating strands by hand. (If using dried noodles, cover with boiling water and soak for 5 minutes; drain, coat with a little oil and set aside.)

5. In a nonstick wok or skillet, heat 1 tbsp (15 mL) of the oil over high heat until just smoking. Add onion, garlic and ginger root; stir-fry until fragrant, about 30 seconds. Add beef mixture and stir-fry until meat is cooked through, about 2 minutes. Transfer to a heatproof dish and keep warm.

6. Add chicken stock and reserved tomato juice to pan and bring to a boil over medium-high heat. Add hoisin sauce and beans; stir, cover and cook for 2 minutes. Add tomatoes and stir for 1 minute. Remove vegetables with a slotted spoon, add to beef mixture and keep warm.

7. Add remaining 1 tbsp (15 mL) oil to liquid in pan. Add noodles and stir-fry until warmed through, about 2 minutes. Transfer to a serving platter. Return beef and vegetable mixture to pan, mix well and cook briefly until sauce is slightly thickened; season to taste with salt and pepper. Pour over noodles and serve immediately.

PEPPERED BEEF WITH FLAT RICE NOODLES

SERVES 4

This Chinese version of pepper steak is one of our family favorites.

For extra spice, add 2 tsp (10 mL) of satay sauce to the sauce mixture.

For variety, we sometimes replace the peppers with shredded cabbage, Napa cabbage or broccoli.

Marinade:

1 tbsp	oyster sauce	15 mL
1 tbsp	soya sauce	15 mL
1 tsp	coarsely ground black pepper	5 mL
2 tbsp	sherry	25 mL
1 1/2 tsp	cornstarch	7 mL
12 oz	sirloin steak, cut into thin strips	375 g

Sauce:

1 tbsp	soya sauce	15 mL
1/4 cup	chicken stock	50 mL
1 lb	fresh flat rice noodles *or* fresh fettuccine	500 g
2 tbsp	vegetable oil	25 mL
3 tbsp	finely chopped shallots	45 mL
1 tbsp	finely chopped ginger root	15 mL
1 tbsp	finely chopped garlic	15 mL
3/4 cup	thinly sliced green bell peppers	175 mL
3/4 cup	thinly sliced red bell peppers	175 mL
1 cup	bean sprouts, packed down	250 mL
	Freshly ground pepper	

1. In a medium-sized bowl, combine ingredients for marinade. Add beef and marinate for 20 minutes.

2. In a small bowl, prepare sauce by combining soya sauce and chicken stock; set aside.

3. If using fresh rice noodles, break them up by placing in a colander, running hot water over them and separating the strands with your fingers. (If using fettuccine, prepare according to package directions, drain and coat with a little oil.)

4. In a nonstick wok or skillet, heat oil over high heat for 30 seconds. Add shallots, ginger root and garlic; stir-fry for 30 seconds. Add beef and stir-fry for 2 minutes, stirring to separate pieces. Add peppers and stir-fry for 2 minutes. Add noodles and sauce, stirring constantly until heated through. Add bean sprouts and mix well. Season to taste with freshly ground pepper and serve immediately.

CRISPY CHOW MEIN WITH A BEEF, TOMATO, LEMON AND HONEY SAUCE

SERVES 4

AS A MAIN COURSE OR

6 AS AN APPETIZER

This interpretation of a classic noodle house dish is one of our favorites. It makes an elegant appetizer for company and the sauce also works well with lamb or seafood (especially shrimp).

The canned tomato juice used here should be a staple in your kitchen. It brings out the flavor of food and adds richness without fat.

Preheat oven to 375°F (190° C)

10-inch (25 cm) ovenproof frying pan (or cast iron skillet) or 13- by 9-inch (3 L) baking dish

1 lb	fresh chow mein noodles	500 g
2 tbsp	vegetable oil, plus oil for coating noodles	25 mL
1 lb	sirloin steak, cut into thin strips	500 g
2 tbsp	cornstarch	25 mL
1 tbsp	minced garlic	15 mL
	Salt and pepper, to taste	
1	onion, sliced	1
	Juice and zest of 1 lemon	
1 tbsp	honey	15 mL
1 tbsp	*char sui* sauce *or* barbecue sauce	15 mL
1 cup	tomato juice	250 mL
1 cup	beef stock	250 mL
2	tomatoes, diced	2
1 tbsp	chopped cilantro	15 mL

1. In a heatproof bowl or pot, cover noodles with boiling water and soak for 5 minutes. Drain, coat with a little oil and set aside.

2. In a nonstick wok or ovenproof skillet, heat 1 tbsp (15 mL) of the oil over medium-high heat for 30 seconds. Add noodles and cook, shaking the pan occasionally, until bottom is crispy and golden brown, about 8 to 10 minutes. Flip noodles over and fluff lightly. Place skillet in oven (or transfer noodles to a baking dish, if using) and bake until noodles are crisp and browned, about 15 minutes.

3. Meanwhile, in a medium-sized bowl, combine cornstarch, garlic, salt and pepper. Add sirloin and mix well.

4. In another nonstick wok or skillet, heat remaining 1 tbsp (15 mL) oil over medium-high heat for 30 seconds. Add beef mixture, and sauté until it browns and begins to crisp. Remove from pan and set aside.

5. Return pan to heat. Add onion and sauté until softened. Add lemon juice and zest, honey, *char sui* sauce, tomato juice, stock and tomatoes; cook for 5 minutes. Add beef and cook until sauce begins to thicken, about 1 or 2 minutes.

6. Remove noodles from the oven and transfer to a large serving platter. Pour sauce over noodles, garnish with cilantro and serve immediately.

THICK RICE NOODLES WITH A BEEF, ONION, CORN AND ROSEMARY SAUCE

SERVES 4

Although this recipe works well with fettuccine, make an effort to find fresh thick rice noodles — they'll meld into the sauce and transform the everyday ingredients into a treasure of comfort food. Be generous with the hot sauce and slurp the noodles up with a fork and spoon.

1 lb	fresh rice noodles *or* fresh fettuccine	500 g
1 tsp	vegetable oil, plus oil for coating noodles	5 mL
8 oz	lean ground beef	250 g
1	onion, diced	1
1 tbsp	finely chopped rosemary	15 mL
1 cup	fresh or frozen corn kernels	250 mL
2 cups	beef or vegetable stock	500 mL
1 tbsp	cornstarch dissolved in 2 tbsp (25 mL) water	15 mL
	Salt and pepper to taste	
	Hot pepper sauce *or* sweet chili sauce	

1. If using fresh noodles, break them up by placing in a colander, running hot water over them and, if necessary, separating the strands with your fingers. (If using pasta, prepare according to package directions, drain and coat with a little oil.)

2. In a nonstick wok or skillet, heat oil over medium-high heat for 30 seconds. Add beef, onions and rosemary. Sauté, stirring often, until beef is well browned. Drain excess fat.

3. Add corn and stock and return to a boil. Add dissolved cornstarch and stir until the sauce begins to thicken. Season to taste with salt and pepper. Add noodles, mix well and heat until the noodles are soft, pliable and heated through, about 2 or 3 minutes. (The dish will benefit from standing for a few minutes with the heat off; be careful not to leave it too long, however, or the noodles will become a starchy mass.) Serve with plenty of hot pepper sauce or sweet chili sauce.

5-SPICE CHICKEN WITH GINGER AND SCALLION LO MEIN (PAGE 137) ➤

OVERLEAF: SHANGHAI NOODLES WITH SHREDDED CHICKEN, CHINESE CABBAGE ➤ AND A SPICY SESAME SAUCE (PAGE 138)

STIR-FRIED LINGUINE WITH LAMB, CHINESE GREENS AND CHILI-PLUM SAUCE

SERVES 4

This dish blends techniques from southern Italy and Szechuan, China. The sumptuous combination of hot chili with sweet plum sauce makes it a clear winner. If you're a lover of spicy food, don't be afraid to turn up the heat a notch — in Szechuan this dish would probably numb your face!

8 oz	dried linguine	250 g
1 tbsp	vegetable oil, plus oil for coating noodles	15 mL
1 tbsp	minced garlic	15 mL
1	onion, thinly sliced	1
8 oz	ground lamb	250 g
4	Chinese broccoli stalks *or* 1 stalk broccoli, thinly sliced	4
4	baby bok choy, shredded *or* 2 cups (500 mL) chopped spinach	500 mL
2 tbsp	plum sauce	25 mL
1 tsp	chili sauce	5 mL
1 tbsp	soya sauce	15 mL
1 1/2 cups	beef stock	375 mL
1 tbsp	cornstarch, dissolved in 2 tbsp (25 mL) water	15 mL
	Salt and pepper	

1. In a large pot of boiling salted water, cook linguine until it is *al dente*, about 8 minutes. Drain, coat with a little oil and set aside.

2. In a nonstick wok or skillet, heat oil over medium-high heat for 30 seconds. Add garlic, onions and lamb; sauté until the lamb is well-cooked. Drain excess fat.

3. Add the broccoli, bok choy, plum sauce, chili sauce, soya sauce and stock to the skillet. Bring mixture to a boil. Add the dissolved cornstarch and stir until the liquid thickens. Add linguine and toss until the pasta is well coated. Season with salt and pepper to taste. Serve immediately.

◄ SATAY-GLAZED VEGETABLE SKEWERS WITH CILANTRO PARMESAN NOODLES (PAGE 153)

VERMICELLI RICE NOODLES WITH A GROUND PORK, CHINESE MUSHROOM, GARLIC AND HOISIN SAUCE

SERVES 4

Hoisin is a sweet and slightly spicy paste, usually made from soya, chilies and yams; it is readily available in the oriental section of most supermarkets. In this quick and delicious dish, hoisin integrates the flavors of the pork and mushrooms.

4	dried Chinese mushrooms	4
8 oz	thin rice vermicelli (thin rice stick noodles) *or* spaghettini	250 g
1 tbsp	vegetable oil, plus oil for coating noodles	15 mL
8 oz	lean ground pork	250 g
1 tsp	minced garlic	5 mL
1 tbsp	chopped cilantro	15 mL
1 tbsp	hoisin sauce	15 mL
1 tbsp	cornstarch dissolved in 2 tbsp (25 mL) water	15 mL
	Salt and pepper to taste	

1. In a heatproof bowl or pot soak mushrooms in 1 cup (250 mL) boiling water for 15 minutes. Drain and reserve liquid. Remove stems and discard. Cut caps into thin slices and return mushrooms to reserved liquid.

2. In a heatproof bowl or pot, cover noodles in boiling water and soak for 3 minutes. (If using pasta, prepare according to package directions.) Drain, toss with a little oil and set aside.

3. In a nonstick wok or skillet, heat oil over medium-high heat for 30 seconds. Add pork and sauté until it begins to brown. Add garlic and cook for 5 minutes. Drain excess fat.

4. Add cilantro, hoisin sauce, mushrooms and reserved liquid (straining out sediment) and heat through. Bring to a boil. Add dissolved cornstarch and stir until the sauce begins to thicken. Add noodles and toss. Season with salt and pepper. Serve immediately.

THIN EGG NOODLES WITH SHREDDED HAM IN A SWEET PEA AND GARLIC CREAM

SERVES 4

Smoked ham works best in this great comfort food dish, but smoked turkey or chicken makes a nice variation.

Use a blender to make smooth cream sauces. When working with hot liquid, however, remember to cover the top of the blender with a folded towel — otherwise you could end up with a burn and a mess.

12 oz	thin egg noodles *or* angel hair pasta	375 g
	Vegetable oil for coating noodles	
3/4 cup	whipping (35%) cream	175 mL
3/4 cup	chicken stock	175 mL
1 cup	fresh or frozen peas	250 mL
1/4 cup	white wine (optional)	50 mL
1 tsp	minced garlic	15 mL
	Salt and pepper to taste	
1/2 cup	shredded ham	125 mL

1. In a large pot of boiling salted water, cook noodles until *al dente*, about 3 to 4 minutes. (If using pasta, prepare according to package directions.) Drain, toss with a little oil and set aside.

2. In a large skillet over high heat, combine whipping cream, stock, peas, white wine, garlic, salt and pepper. Bring to a boil and immediately reduce heat to medium. Simmer for 2 minutes, or until the peas are tender. Remove from heat.

3. Transfer pea mixture to a blender or food processor, filling no further than the halfway point. Process until the mixture is a smooth, pale green. Repeat, if necessary.

4. Return sauce to skillet. Add the ham and noodles; stir to coat and gently heat through. Serve immediately.

LEMON GRASS PORK CHOPS WITH CHINESE PESTO NOODLES

SERVES 4

The trick to this dish is having the noodles ready just as the chops finish cooking.

A simple green salad or some pickled vegetables is all you need for a great meal.

Preheat broiler or, if using, start barbecue

Marinade:

1 tbsp	minced garlic	15 mL
1 tbsp	minced ginger root	15 mL
1 tbsp	brown sugar	15 mL
1/4 tsp	HOME-STYLE 5-SPICE MIX (see recipe, page 28) *or* commercially prepared 5-spice powder	1 mL
1 tbsp	sherry, optional	15 mL
1	lemon grass stalk, smashed and chopped, *or* 2 tsp (10 mL) lemon zest	1
4	pork chops, each about 6 oz (150 g)	4
1 tsp	sesame oil	5 mL
1	small chili, seeded and finely chopped	1
1 tbsp	honey	15 mL
8 oz	broad vermicelli (broad rice stick noodles) *or* fettuccine	250 g
1 cup	CHINESE PESTO (see recipe, page 171)	250 mL

1. In a small bowl, combine ingredients for marinade. Place pork chops in a dish and spread marinade evenly over them. Cover and marinate, refrigerated, for 4 hours or overnight. Remove from refrigerator 30 minutes before cooking.

2. In a small bowl, combine sesame oil, chili and honey. Set aside.

3. Broil or grill one side of pork chops until golden brown, about 6 minutes. Baste cooked side with sesame oil mixture and continue cooking for 1 minute. Flip chops over and repeat cooking/basting procedure. The chops should be slightly charred but not burnt.

4. Just before the chops are ready, cook noodles in a large pot of boiling water for 2 minutes. Remove from heat and let soak for 5 minutes. (If using pasta, prepare according to package directions.) Drain, transfer to large bowl, add CHINESE PESTO and toss to mix well.

5. Divide noodles into serving portions. Top each with a pork chop and serve immediately.

THICK EGG NOODLES WITH BARBECUED PORK, ONION, GREEN PEPPER AND BLACK BEAN SAUCE

SERVES 4

If there's Chinatown near you, barbecued pork is a treat you can pick up on your way home from work. Team it up with some vegetables and noodles and you have an instant meal.

This recipe also works well with roast beef or leftover lamb.

8 oz	dried thick egg noodles *or* fettuccine	250 g
1 tbsp	vegetable oil, plus oil for coating noodles	15 mL
1	onion, thinly sliced	1
1	green pepper, seeded and sliced	1
1 tbsp	minced garlic	15 mL
1 tbsp	minced ginger root	15 mL
2 tbsp	black bean sauce	25 mL
1 tsp	chili paste	5 mL
2 cups	chicken stock	500 mL
1 tbsp	cornstarch dissolved in 2 tbsp (25 mL) water	15 mL
8 oz	barbecued pork, shredded	250 g
1 cup	bean sprouts	250 mL

1. In a large pot of boiling salted water, cook noodles until *al dente*, about 4 or 5 minutes. (If using pasta, prepare according to package directions.) Drain, coat with a little oil and set aside.

2. In a nonstick wok or skillet, heat oil over medium-high heat for 30 seconds. Add onion, pepper, garlic and ginger root; sauté for 2 to 3 minutes or until the onion softens and begins to color. Add black bean sauce, chili paste and chicken stock. Bring mixture to a boil. Add the dissolved cornstarch and stir until the sauce thickens.

3. Add pork, bean sprouts and noodles. Heat through for 1 or 2 minutes and serve immediately.

POULTRY

SOBA NOODLES STIR-FRIED WITH CHICKEN, PEAS, GARLIC AND BASIL

SERVES 4

Soba noodles are made from buckwheat and packed with fiber and nutrients. The chicken makes this a very nutritious one-dish meal.

If you're feeling decadent and want to undermine the health benefits, add 1/2 cup (125 mL) whipping (35%) cream along with the white wine.

8 oz	dried Soba noodles *or* whole-wheat spaghetti	250 g
1 tbsp	vegetable oil, plus oil for coating noodles	15 mL
8 oz	boneless chicken breast	250 g
1/2 tsp	salt	2 mL
1/2 tsp	pepper	2 mL
1 tbsp	minced garlic	15 mL
1 cup	frozen peas	250 mL
3 tbsp	white wine	45 mL
1 tbsp	finely chopped fresh basil	15 mL
1 tbsp	extra virgin olive oil	15 mL
2 tbsp	grated Parmesan cheese	25 mL

1. In a large pot of boiling salted water, cook noodles until *al dente*, about 6 to 8 minutes. Drain, coat with a little oil and set aside.

2. On a cutting board, cut chicken into 1-inch (2.5 cm) slices and cut each slice into thin strips. Season with salt and pepper; set aside.

3. In a nonstick wok or skillet, heat oil over medium-high heat for 30 seconds. Add garlic and chicken; sauté until the chicken begins to brown. Add peas and wine; simmer for 4 to 5 minutes. Add basil, noodles, olive oil and Parmesan. Mix well and serve immediately.

5-SPICE CHICKEN WITH GINGER AND SCALLION LO MEIN

SERVES 4

This is basically a roasted version of the poached soya chicken so popular in Chinese noodle shops. Roasting gives the chicken a more concentrated flavor. It's delicious with ginger and scallions.

Preheat oven to 375° F (190° C)

1/2 tsp	HOME-STYLE 5-SPICE MIX (see recipe, page 28) *or* commercially prepared 5-spice powder	2 mL
1/2 tsp	freshly ground black pepper	2 mL
1 tbsp	coarsely chopped garlic	15 mL
1 tbsp	brown sugar	15 mL
1 tbsp	dark soya sauce *or* mushroom soya sauce	15 mL
1 tbsp	fish sauce	15 mL
1 tsp	sesame oil	5 mL
2	large chicken breasts	2
1	recipe GINGER AND SCALLION LO MEIN (see page 170)	1

1. In a small bowl, combine 5-spice, pepper, garlic, sugar, soya sauce, fish sauce and sesame oil; mix well. Rub marinade evenly over chicken; cover and refrigerate for 4 hours or overnight, turning occasionally.

2. Place chicken in roasting pan and pour any residual marinade over the chicken. Roast for 20 minutes, then baste with pan drippings. Continue cooking for an additional 10 minutes or until liquid runs clear when the thickest part of the breast is pierced with a fork. If necessary, turn the broiler on and brown the chicken on each side until it is crisp (being careful not to burn, which happens quickly) about 1 minute per side.

3. Meanwhile, prepare GINGER SCALLION LO MEIN up to the point of cooking the noodles. Keep a pot of boiling water ready for the noodles.

4. Remove chicken from oven. Allow to rest for 2 minutes, then divide into 4 portions. Complete GINGER SCALLION LO MEIN and serve as an accompaniment.

SHANGHAI NOODLES WITH SHREDDED CHICKEN, CHINESE CABBAGE AND A SPICY SESAME SAUCE

SERVES 4

A traditional version of this dish would consist of shredded beef and Chinese cabbage tossed with soya sauce. For a change of pace we've used chicken breast and spiced up the sauce with chili paste and sesame seeds.

Shred cabbage by cutting into thin strips, starting at the tip of the leaves. If using a green cabbage cut the head in quarters, remove core and shred.

1 lb	fresh Shanghai noodles or 8 oz (250 g) dried spaghetti	500 g
1 tbsp	vegetable oil, plus oil for coating noodles	15 mL
8 oz	boneless, skinless chicken breast	250 g
2 tbsp	cornstarch	25 mL
3 cups	shredded Chinese cabbage or green cabbage	750 mL
1 tsp	minced ginger root	5 mL
1 tsp	minced garlic	5 mL
2 tbsp	water	25 mL
1 tbsp	dark soya sauce	15 mL
1 tbsp	chopped cilantro	15 mL
1 tsp	chili paste (or to taste)	5 mL
1 tsp	sesame oil	5 mL
1 tbsp	toasted sesame seeds, plus extra seeds for garnish	15 mL
	Sliced green onion for garnish	

1. In a heatproof bowl or pot, cover noodles with boiling water and soak for 5 minutes. (If using pasta, prepare according to package directions.) Drain, toss with a little oil and set aside.

2. On a cutting board, cut chicken into thin slices and then cut each slice into thin strips. Dredge strips in cornstarch, shaking off excess starch. Set aside.

3. In a nonstick wok or skillet, heat oil over medium-high heat for 30 seconds. Add ginger root and cook until it starts to sizzle. Add chicken and sauté until brown, about 4 to 5 minutes. Add cabbage and garlic and stir-fry until cabbage is wilted. Add water. Cook, covered, over low heat for 2 minutes.

4. Add soya sauce, cilantro, chili paste, sesame oil and sesame seeds to the mixture; toss well. Garnish with green onions and additional sesame seeds, if desired. Serve immediately.

ORANGE-GLAZED CHICKEN WITH SHANGHAI NOODLES IN PECAN SCALLION SAUCE

SERVES 4

If you like quail, substitute 8 quail for the chicken and you'll have a memorable dish. Butterfly the quail by splitting along the back-bone and removing backbone and neck. On a work surface, place bird bone-side down and press on skin to flatten. Marinate and grill as described in the recipe, but only cook 3 to 4 minutes per side.

Preheat broiler or, if using, start barbecue

Marinade:

1 tbsp	grated ginger root	15 mL
2	green onions, finely chopped	2
2 tbsp	minced garlic	25 mL
4 tbsp	soya sauce	60 mL
2 tsp	grated orange zest	10 mL
2 tbsp	orange juice concentrate	25 mL
2 tbsp	sake or white wine	25 mL
1 tsp	HOME-STYLE 5-SPICE MIX (see recipe, page 28) or commercially prepared 5-spice powder	5 mL
1 tsp	dried chili flakes	5 mL
2 tbsp	honey or brown sugar	25 mL
4	chicken breasts, split	4
1	orange, thinly sliced	1
1 lb	Shanghai noodles	500 g
1	recipe PECAN SCALLION SAUCE (see recipe, page 172)	1

1. In small saucepan over low heat, combine ingredients for marinade; stir until well mixed.

2. Put marinade and chicken in a large freezer or zip-lock bag. Squeeze to remove all air and seal. Rub marinade thoroughly onto chicken through freezer bag and refrigerate for 2 hours or overnight.

3. Prepare PECAN SCALLION SAUCE.

4. Remove chicken from bag and place on barbecue skin-side down (or under broiler skin-side up.) Baste with marinade and cook until golden brown, about 10 minutes. Turn, baste and cook for another 10 minutes, or until juices run clear.

5. Meanwhile, in a large pot of boiling salted water, cook noodles until *al dente*, about 4 to 5 minutes. Drain and transfer to mixing bowl. Add PECAN SCALLION SAUCE to taste; toss and keep warm.

6. Transfer noodles to a platter, top with chicken and garnish with orange slices. Serve immediately.

GINGER TERIYAKI CHICKEN WITH STEAMED RICE NOODLE CAKES

SERVES 4

A salad dressed with
NUOC CHAM (see recipe,
page 33) and cilantro
makes a wonderful
accompaniment to this
delicious Japanese-
inspired dish.

Teriyaki Sauce:

1/4 cup	sake or dry white wine	50 mL
1/4 cup	*mirin* or 2 tbsp (25 mL) honey mixed with 2 tbsp (25 mL) sherry	50 mL
1/4 cup	dark soya sauce	50 mL
2 tsp	sugar	10 mL
1 tbsp	minced ginger root	15 mL
	Vegetable spray	
4	boneless chicken thighs or breasts, skin on	4
	Freshly ground black pepper to taste	
1	recipe STEAMED RICE NOODLE CAKE (see page 167)	1

1. In a small bowl, combine sauce ingredients and set aside.

2. In a nonstick wok or skillet sprayed with vegetable spray, cook chicken, skin-side down, until skin is brown and crisp, about 5 minutes. Turn and cook until chicken is cooked through, about 7 minutes. Remove from pan and set aside. Drain excess oil.

3. Add sauce mixture to skillet and bring to a boil over medium heat, stirring constantly, until sauce begins to thicken, about 2 minutes.

4. Return chicken to skillet; increase heat to high and cook, turning chicken until well-coated with sauce. (Watch carefully to avoid burning.) When almost all the sauce is absorbed, remove chicken; season it with pepper and cut into 1/2-inch (1 cm) slices. Serve over warm STEAMED RICE NOODLE CAKE.

EGG-FRIED CHICKEN WITH GAILAN AND OYSTER SAUCE LO MEIN

SERVES 4 TO 6

Substitute other fresh herbs, such as basil or cilantro, for the parsley.

Any firm white fish — or even butterflied shrimp — makes a delicious substitution for the chicken.

To make the chicken easier to cut, place in the freezer for about 1 hour until it's partially frozen and just firm.

Marinade:

2 tsp	minced garlic	10 mL
2 tsp	minced ginger root	10 mL
2 tbsp	chopped Italian parsley *or* chopped green onions	25 mL
1 tbsp	Chinese cooking wine *or* dry sherry	15 mL
1 tbsp	fish sauce	15 mL
1 tsp	sesame oil	5 mL
1	recipe GAILAN AND OYSTER SAUCE LO MEIN (see page 165)	1
1 lb	boneless chicken breast, cut diagonally into large thin slices	500 g
1/2 cup	cornstarch	125 mL
1 tsp	seasoning salt	5 mL
1 tsp	ground white pepper	5 mL
3	large eggs, beaten	3
3 tbsp	vegetable oil	45 mL

1. In a small bowl combine ingredients for marinade. Add chicken, mix well and set aside for 10 minutes.

2. Prepare GAILAN AND OYSTER SAUCE LO MEIN; keep warm.

3. Combine cornstarch and salt and pepper in a shallow bowl. Dredge pieces of chicken in mixture until lightly and evenly coated, then in eggs until well coated.

4. In a nonstick wok or skillet, heat oil over medium-high heat until just smoking. Add 1 tbsp (15 mL) of the oil and swirl to coat skillet. Add several pieces of chicken and fry until golden, about 1 to 2 minutes per side. Remove chicken and keep warm in oven. Repeat procedure for remaining chicken, adding oil as needed. Serve with GAILAN AND OYSTER SAUCE LO MEIN.

THIN EGG NOODLES WITH A GROUND TURKEY, SESAME, APPLE AND GINGER SAUCE

SERVES 4

Turkey is a lean and flavorful meat which blends well with the sweetness of apple, ginger and a finish of hot pepper

Use canned or bottled applesauce, or make your own by simmering 2 apples (peeled, cored and diced) with a little water until it forms a sauce.

12 oz	dried thin egg noodles or linguine	375 g
1 tbsp	vegetable oil, plus oil for coating noodles	15 mL
1 tbsp	minced ginger root	15 mL
8 oz	ground turkey	250 g
1	red pepper, seeded and shredded	1
1 cup	unsweetened applesauce	250 mL
3 tbsp	chicken stock *or* apple juice	45 mL
1 tsp	sesame oil	5 mL
	Hot pepper sauce *or* chili sauce, to taste	
	Salt and pepper to taste	
1 tbsp	toasted sesame seeds	15 mL

1. In a large pot of boiling salted water, cook noodles or linguine until *al dente*, about 6 minutes. Drain, coat with a little oil and set aside.

2. In a nonstick wok or skillet, heat oil over medium heat for 30 seconds. Add ginger root, turkey and red pepper. Sauté until turkey is cooked and beginning to brown. Add the applesauce, stock and sesame oil. Season to taste with hot sauce and salt and pepper.

3. Add noodles and heat until warmed through, about 1 or 2 minutes. Sprinkle with sesame seeds and serve immediately, with additional hot sauce, if desired.

SHREDDED BARBECUED DUCK AND LEEKS OVER THIN WHEAT NOODLES

SERVES 4

The intense flavor of the duck adds interest to this dish, but results are equally good when it's made with leftover chicken or turkey.

To add some crunch, top with roasted peanuts and bean sprouts.

1 lb	fresh thin wheat noodles or fresh linguine	500 g
1 tbsp	vegetable oil, plus oil for coating noodles	15 mL
4	leeks, white part only	4
1	green pepper, seeded and thinly sliced	1
1 tbsp	minced garlic	15 mL
1 tbsp	*char sui* sauce *or* barbecue sauce	15 mL
1 tbsp	tomato paste *or* ketchup	15 mL
2 cups	chicken stock	500 mL
1 cup	shredded barbecued duck *or* roast chicken *or* turkey	250 mL
1 tbsp	cornstarch dissolved in 2 tbsp (25 mL) water	15 mL
	Roasted peanuts to taste (optional)	
	Bean sprouts to taste (optional)	

1. In a large pot of boiling salted water, cook noodles until *al dente*, about 4 to 5 minutes. (If using pasta, prepare according to package directions.) Drain, toss with a little oil and set aside.

2. Prepare leeks by cutting off root ends and splitting in half, lengthwise. Remove hard core and discard. Rinse well with cold water, flatten on a cutting board and cut into long, thin strips.

3. In a nonstick wok or skillet, heat oil over medium-high heat for 30 seconds. Add leeks, pepper and garlic. Sauté until leek softens, about 1 to 2 minutes. Add *char sui* sauce, tomato paste and chicken stock. Bring to a boil. Add the dissolved cornstarch and stir until mixture thickens. Add duck and noodles; stir to combine and heat through. Garnish with peanuts and/or bean sprouts, if desired. Serve immediately.

PAN-ROASTED DUCK BREAST WITH CHINESE NOODLE ROSTI

SERVES 4

If you like Chinese barbecued duck you'll love this homemade version. (It's also also great with pork tenderloin.)

Marinating is easy with the freezer bag method used here. If you remove as much air as possible from the bag, the marinade will coat the meats quite naturally.

Preheat oven to 400° F (200° C)
Ovenproof skillet or roasting pan

Marinade:

2 tsp	finely grated ginger root	10 mL
1 tsp	minced garlic	5 mL
1 tsp	HOME-STYLE 5-SPICE MIX (see recipe, page 28) or commercially prepared 5-spice powder	5 mL
1 tbsp	hoisin sauce	15 mL
1 tbsp	soya sauce	15 mL
1/4 tsp	salt	1 mL
1 tbsp	sherry	15 mL
1 tbsp	honey	15 mL
1 1/2 tsp	sesame oil	7 mL
1 tbsp	water or chicken stock	15 mL
4	boneless duck breasts or 1 pork tenderloin (about 1 lb [500 g])	4
1	recipe CHINESE NOODLE AND SCALLION ROSTI (see page 166) or GINGER SCALLION LO MEIN (see page 170)	1

1. In a small saucepan over low heat, combine ingredients for marinade, stirring, until honey is melted and well combined. Allow to cool.

2. Put marinade and duck in a large freezer or zip-lock bag. Squeeze to remove all air and seal. Rub marinade thoroughly onto duck through freezer bag and refrigerate for 4 hours or overnight.

3. Remove meat from marinade and reserve marinade for basting. Prick duck skin with fork several times. In a nonstick ovenproof skillet over medium-high heat, fry duck breast skin-side down until golden brown, about 2 minutes. (If using pork, brown one side.) Drain excess fat. Turn and brown other side for about 2 minutes.

4. Baste both sides of meat with marinade. Place pan in heated oven and roast for 15 minutes. (Duck should be skin side up.)

5. Meanwhile, prepare noodle recipe and keep warm.

6. Remove meat from oven and let rest for 5 minutes. Cut into bite-sized slices and serve over noodles accompanied by a green salad.

$\mathcal{V}$EGETABLES

OVEN-ROASTED CHOW MEIN WITH MIXED HERBS, OLIVE OIL AND GARLIC

SERVES 4

AS A MAIN COURSE OR 6 TO 8 AS A SIDE DISH

Crispy wisps of oven-roasted chow mein enhance any meal, especially with an accent of garlic and fresh herbs. If you're using dry herbs use only the suggested amounts — their flavor is very concentrated.

Preheat oven to 350° F (180° C)
Ovenproof skillet or 13- by 9-inch (3 L) baking dish

1 lb	fresh chow mein noodles	500 g
2 tbsp	olive oil, plus oil for coating noodles	25 mL
1 tbsp	minced garlic	15 mL
1 tbsp	finely chopped fresh basil (or 1/2 tsp [2 mL] dried)	15 mL
1 tsp	finely chopped rosemary (fresh or dried)	5 mL
1 tsp	finely chopped sage (or pinch dried)	5 mL
	Salt and pepper	

1. In a heatproof bowl or pot, cover noodles with boiling water and soak for 5 minutes. Drain and toss with a little oil.

2. In an ovenproof skillet, heat oil for 30 seconds. Add noodles and stir-fry until well coated. Sprinkle with garlic and herbs. Season with salt and pepper; mix well.

3. Place skillet in oven (or transfer to baking dish, if using) and roast for 15 minutes or until noodles are crisp and golden. Serve immediately.

THIN RICE NOODLES WITH CAULIFLOWER AND BLACK BEAN SAUCE

SERVES 4

AS A MAIN COURSE OR

6 TO 8 AS A SIDE DISH

The pungent, earthy flavor of black beans makes this a hearty and satisfying vegetarian dish.

Pre-steaming the cauliflower gives a soft and luxurious feel. For a crunchier texture, thinly slice raw cauliflower and sauté along with the onion.

8 oz	thin rice vermicelli (thin rice stick noodles) *or* dried linguine	250 g
1 tbsp	vegetable oil, plus oil for coating noodles	15 mL
2 cups	cauliflower florets	500 mL
1 tbsp	minced garlic	15 mL
1 tbsp	minced ginger root	15 mL
1	onion, coarsely chopped	1
1	green pepper, seeded and thinly sliced	1
2 tbsp	black bean sauce	25 mL
2 cups	water *or* chicken or beef stock	500 mL
1 tbsp	cornstarch dissolved in 2 tbsp (25 mL) water	15 mL

1. In a heatproof bowl or pot, cover noodles with boiling water and soak for 3 minutes. (If using pasta, prepare according to package directions.) Drain, coat with a little oil and set aside.

2. In a colander, rinse cauliflower under cold water. Transfer to a steamer and cook for 5 minutes (or microwave in a covered container with 2 tbsp [25 mL] water for 4 minutes) until tender but slightly firm. Set aside.

3. In a nonstick wok or skillet, heat oil over medium-high heat for 30 seconds. Add garlic, ginger root, onion, pepper and cauliflower. Sauté for 2 minutes or until onion softens. Add black bean sauce and stir. Add water or stock and cook for another 2 minutes. Add dissolved cornstarch and stir to thicken. Add noodles, mix well and cook 1 minute to warm through. Serve immediately.

BAKED RICE NOODLE ROLLS WITH MUSHROOMS, OLIVES AND A HERBED TOMATO SAUCE

SERVES 4

You can buy thick sheets of flat rice noodles (similar to lasagna) in Asian markets.

Typically, a filling such as barbecued pork or shrimp is rolled up in the noodle and the package is gently steamed. Here the noodle sheets are baked like lasagna, but the texture is more melt-in-the-mouth than the Italian version.

Preheat oven to 350° F (180° C)
9- by 13-inch (3 L) ovenproof casserole dish greased with olive oil

1	can (28 oz [796 mL]) tomatoes	1
2 tbsp	olive oil *or* vegetable oil	25 mL
1	onion, diced	1
2 cups	sliced mushrooms	500 mL
2	cloves garlic, minced	2
1/4 cup	pitted, coarsely chopped green olives	50 mL
1 tbsp	chopped fresh marjoram (or 1/2 tsp [2 mL] dried)	15 mL
1 tbsp	chopped rosemary (fresh or dried)	15 mL
	Salt and pepper to taste	
1 lb	fresh rice noodle rolls *or* cooked lasagna sheets	500 g
2 cups	shredded skim mozzarella cheese	500 mL

1. In a medium-sized bowl, crush tomatoes with a fork (or pulse in a food processor) until they are in bite-size pieces. Set aside.

2. In a nonstick wok or skillet, heat oil over medium-high heat for 30 seconds. Add onions and sauté until they begin to color. Add mushrooms and garlic and cook until mushrooms begin to soften. Stir in tomatoes, olives, marjoram and rosemary; season with salt and pepper and bring to a simmer. Cook for 3 minutes.

3. Spread 1/4 cup (50 mL) of sauce evenly over bottom of prepared dish, then unroll 3 noodle sheets over sauce. Top with one third of the sauce and an equal amount of cheese. Repeat with remaining sauce and sheets until you have 3 layers. Bake for 30 minutes or until top is golden brown. Let rest for 3 to 4 minutes before serving.

SATAY-GLAZED VEGETABLE SKEWERS WITH CILANTRO PARMESAN NOODLES

SERVES 4

Satay sauce, sometimes labeled barbecue sauce, is a pantry favorite which can be used to give almost anything a lift — from meats and seafood, to vegetables.

Preheat broiler or, if using, start barbecue

2	zucchini, cut into a total of 16 slices, each 1 inch (2.5 cm) thick	2
2	red bell peppers, cut into a total of 16 large squares	2
16	large mushrooms	16
8	bamboo skewers, soaked in water for 4 hours	8
2 tbsp	olive oil	25 mL

Basting Sauce:

1 tbsp	satay sauce (Chinese barbecue sauce)	15 mL
1 tbsp	honey	15 mL
1 tbsp	hoisin sauce	15 mL
1 tbsp	soya sauce	15 mL
1 tbsp	balsamic vinegar	15 mL
1	recipe CILANTRO PARMESAN NOODLES (see recipe, page 169)	1

1. Thread skewers in an attractive arrangement, using 2 pieces of each vegetable for each skewer.

2. In a small bowl, combine ingredients for basting sauce and mix well.

3. Prepare CILANTRO PARMESAN NOODLES and keep warm.

4. Brush vegetable skewers with olive oil and grill or broil 1 minute on each side. Baste each side with sauce and continue cooking for another 2 minutes on each side or until vegetables are just tender. Continue to baste during cooking to ensure that the vegetables are well coated and seasoned.

5. Divide CILANTRO PARMESAN NOODLES between 4 plates. Top with cooked vegetables; serve immediately.

CRISPY CHOW MEIN NOODLES WITH CHINESE MUSHROOMS AND GREENS

SERVES 4

We make this dish with dried Chinese mushrooms, but you can substitute fresh mushrooms such as button, shiitake or oyster.

Wood ear fungus is a type of mushroom found in Asian markets. It provides a unique texture to this dish.

You can also substitute chicken stock for the mushroom soaking liquid.

Preheat oven to 375° F (190° C)
10-inch (25 cm) ovenproof frying pan (or cast iron skillet),
or 9 -by 13-inch (3 L) baking dish

8	dried shiitake mushrooms *or* morels *or* any other type of dried mushroom	8
2	dried wood ear fungus *or* fresh oyster mushrooms	2
1	can 15 oz (425 mL) straw mushrooms *or* 1 lb (500 g) fresh button mushrooms	1
1 lb	fresh chow mein noodles	500 g
2 tbsp	vegetable oil, plus oil for coating noodles	25 mL
4	whole green onions, cut into 1-inch (2.5 cm) pieces	4
1 tbsp	minced garlic	15 mL
1 cup	mushroom soaking liquid *or* chicken stock	250 mL
4	baby bok choy, quartered *or* 2 cups (500 mL) chopped fresh spinach	4
4	stalks Chinese broccoli *or* 1 stalk broccoli	4
	Sesame oil	
1 tbsp	dark soya sauce	15 mL
1 tbsp	cornstarch dissolved in 2 tbsp [25 mL] water	15 mL
	Salt and pepper, to taste	

1. In a heatproof bowl or pot, soak dried mushrooms in 2 cups (500 mL) boiling water for 15 minutes. Drain and reserve liquid. Remove thick stems from wood ear fungus and cut into a fine shred. Discard tough stems from the black mushrooms and cut each cap in quarters. Return mushrooms to soaking liquid.

2. Drain straw mushrooms and rinse with cold water. Set aside. (If using fresh mushrooms, cut them into quarters; set aside.)

3. In a heatproof bowl or pot, cover noodles with boiling water and soak for 5 minutes. Drain, toss with a little vegetable oil and set aside.

4. In a nonstick wok or skillet, heat 1 tbsp (15 mL) oil over high heat for 30 seconds. Add noodles and reduce heat to medium; cook, shaking the pan occasionally, until bottom is golden brown, about 8 to 10 minutes. Flip noodles over and fluff lightly. Place skillet in oven (or transfer noodles to a baking dish, if using) and bake until noodles are crisp and browned, about 15 minutes.

5. Meanwhile, heat remaining oil in another skillet over high heat for 30 seconds. Add onions and garlic. When onion starts to soften, add straw mushrooms (or fresh, if using), broccoli, bok choy and sauté for 3 to 4 minutes. Add remaining mushrooms and their liquid, leaving any sediment behind. Add sesame oil and soya sauce. Bring to a boil. Add dissolved cornstarch and stir until thickened. Season to taste with salt and pepper.

6. Remove noodles from oven and transfer to a deep serving plate. Pour mushroom sauce over top and serve immediately.

THIN WHEAT NOODLES STIR-FRIED WITH MIXED PEPPERS, SOYA AND GINGER

SERVES 4

This is a simple and satisfying combination of sweet peppers and Asian spices.

Try adding a small handful of your favorite herbs along with the soya sauce and serve with extra soya and some hot sauce at the table.

1 lb	fresh thin wheat noodles, such as wunton or linguine	500 g
1 tbsp	olive oil	15 mL
1	onion, thinly sliced	1
1 tbsp	minced ginger	15 mL
1 tsp	minced garlic	5 mL
1	red pepper, seeded and sliced	1
1	yellow pepper, seeded and sliced	1
1	green pepper, seeded and sliced	1
1 tbsp	soya sauce	15 mL
	Salt and pepper	

1. In a large pot of boiling salted water, cook noodles until *al dente*, about 3 to 4 minutes. (If using pasta, prepare according to package directions.) Drain, coat with a little oil, and set aside.

2. In a nonstick wok or skillet, heat oil over medium-high heat for 30 seconds. Add onion, ginger and garlic. Sauté until the onion begins to soften and color. Add mixed peppers and sauté for 4 to 5 minutes or until the peppers begin to soften. Season to taste with salt and pepper.

3. Add drained noodles and soya sauce to mixture. Toss well and heat through, about 1 to 2 minutes. Serve immediately.

STIR-FRIED THICK RICE NOODLES WITH SPICED EGGPLANT, TOMATO, GARLIC AND CILANTRO

SERVES 4

Fresh, thick, round rice noodles — often called lai fen — are usually sold in vacuum packs in Asian specialty stores. With spiced, baked eggplant, they make a robust dish.

Preheat oven to 375° F (190° C)
Greased baking sheet

Spiced Eggplant:

1	eggplant, cut into 2-inch (5 cm) cubes	1
1 tbsp	minced garlic	15 mL
1 tsp	chili paste	5 mL
	Salt and pepper to taste	
2 tbsp	olive oil	25 mL
1 lb	fresh broad rice noodles *or* fresh spaghetti	500 g
1 tbsp	olive oil, plus oil for coating noodles	15 mL
1 tsp	minced garlic	5 mL
1 tbsp	chopped cilantro	15 mL
2	tomatoes, diced	2
1/4 cup	grated Parmesan cheese	50 mL

1. In a mixing bowl combine eggplant, garlic, chili paste, salt, pepper, and olive oil; mix well. Transfer to prepared baking sheet and bake for 20 minutes or until eggplant is soft and lightly browned. Set aside.

2. In a large pot of boiling salted water, cook noodles until *al dente*, about 4 to 5 minutes. (If using pasta, prepare according to package directions.) Drain, coat with a little vegetable oil, and set aside.

3. In a nonstick wok or skillet, heat oil over medium-high heat for 30 seconds. Add garlic, cilantro and tomatoes. Add eggplant mixture and cook until tomatoes are warmed through. Add noodles and toss well. Add half the Parmesan and toss. Transfer to a serving dish, sprinkle with remaining cheese and serve immediately.

SOY-BRAISED TOFU, CABBAGE AND GINGER WITH CELLOPHANE NOODLES

SERVES 4

Braising is a key component of Chinese cooking — it adds rich flavor to otherwise bland ingredients such as tofu. Baking also firms the tofu and allows the flavorings to penetrate.

For added flavor, roast the cabbage along with the tofu.

Bean thread noodles are very slippery and best eaten with chopsticks.

Preheat oven to 375° F (190° C)
Greased baking sheet

4 oz	bean thread noodles *or* 8 oz (250 g) dried angel hair pasta	125 g
1 tbsp	vegetable oil, plus oil for coating noodles	15 mL
4 oz	medium-firm tofu, cut into 1/2-inch (1 cm) cubes	125 g
2 tbsp	soya sauce	25 mL
2 tbsp	minced ginger root	25 mL
1 tbsp	minced garlic	15 mL
4 cups	vegetable stock *or* apple juice	1 L
2 cups	shredded green cabbage	500 mL
1 tbsp	chopped cilantro	15 mL
2 tbsp	tomato ketchup	25 mL
1 tbsp	horseradish	15 mL
1 tbsp	cornstarch dissolved in 2 tbsp (25 mL)water	15 mL
	Salt and pepper to taste	

1. In a heatproof bowl or pot, cover noodles with boiling water and soak for 3 minutes. Drain. (If using pasta, prepare according to package directions, and coat with a little oil.) Set aside.

2. In a large bowl combine tofu, oil, soya sauce, ginger and garlic. Place on a baking sheet and roast until firm and browned, about 15 minutes. Remove from oven and allow to cool slightly.

3. Meanwhile, in a saucepan over medium-high heat, combine stock, cabbage, tofu mixture, cilantro, ketchup and horseradish. Bring to a boil. Reduce heat and simmer for 5 minutes. Add dissolved cornstarch and cook until mixture begins to thicken. Add noodles and stir until heated through. Season with salt and pepper; serve immediately.

STIR-FRIED WUNTON NOODLES WITH ROASTED PEPPERS AND GARLIC

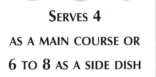

SERVES 4
AS A MAIN COURSE OR
6 TO 8 AS A SIDE DISH

Roasted peppers are a sensual treat, and they're now available throughout the year.

Fresh wunton noodles are available in Chinese grocers. They are very fine and require surprisingly little cooking time.

Preheat oven to 375° F (190° C)
Baking sheet

4	red peppers, seeded and halved	4
2	heads garlic	2
1 tbsp	olive oil	15 mL
	Salt and pepper to taste	
1 lb	fresh wunton noodles *or* 8 oz (250 g) dried spaghettini	500 g
2 tbsp	olive oil	25 mL
1 tbsp	toasted sesame seeds	15 mL

1. Coat peppers with oil and season with salt and pepper. Cut top third off garlic heads, drizzle with oil and season with salt and pepper. On a baking sheet, roast garlic and peppers in preheated oven for 30 minutes or until peppers are browned and slightly shriveled.

2. Transfer roasted peppers to a large mixing bowl and cover with plastic film. Let peppers rest for 10 minutes. Peel peppers (the skin should lift off easily) and cut into julienne strips; set aside. Squeeze garlic cloves to extract paste; discard the skin.

3. In a nonstick wok or skillet over medium heat, toss peppers, garlic paste and olive oil until well combined. Set aside.

4. In a large pot of boiling salted water, cook noodles until *al dente*, about 1 to 2 minutes. (If using pasta, prepare according to package directions.) Drain, shake off excess moisture and add to pan. Toss until well mixed and heat to warm through. Season with salt and pepper. Garnish with sesame seeds and serve immediately.

RICE STICK NOODLES WITH SWEET-AND-SOUR TOMATO, CILANTRO AND GINGER SAUCE

SERVES 4

This is a delicious version of the old standby, sweet-and-sour sauce. Resembling a chunky chutney, it keeps well in a jar in the fridge or frozen in zip-lock bags.

For a real treat, try adding a handful of raw shrimp to the hot sauce and cook until they just turn pink (about 4 minutes).

8 oz	thin rice vermicelli (thin rice stick noodles) *or* angel hair pasta	250 g
1 tbsp	vegetable oil, plus oil for coating noodles	15 mL
1	can (19 oz [398 mL]) tomatoes, including juice	1
1	onion, diced	1
1	stalk celery, finely diced	1
2 tbsp	minced ginger root	25 mL
4	cloves	4
1 cup	tomato juice	250 mL
2 tbsp	rice vinegar	25 mL
2 tbsp	honey	25 mL
1 tsp	ground allspice	5 mL
1 tsp	chili paste	5 mL
1 tbsp	cornstarch dissolved in 2 tbsp (25 mL) water	15 mL
1 tbsp	chopped cilantro	15 mL
	Salt and pepper to taste	

1. In a heatproof bowl or pot, cover noodles with boiling water and soak for 3 minutes. (If using pasta, prepare according to package directions.) Drain, coat with a little oil and set aside.

2. In a mixing bowl, crush tomatoes with a fork or process briefly in a food processor until coarsely chopped.

THIN WHEAT NOODLES STIR-FRIED WITH MIXED PEPPERS, SOYA AND GINGER (PAGE 156) ➤

3. In a large saucepan heat oil over medium-high heat for 30 seconds. Add onion, celery, ginger and cloves; sauté 3 to 4 minutes or until the onion has softened and is beginning to color. Add tomato juice and crushed tomatoes with juice. Bring to a boil. Add vinegar, honey, allspice and chili paste. Return to a boil and add dissolved cornstarch, stirring until the sauce begins to thicken, about 3 minutes. Season to taste with salt and pepper.

4. In a serving bowl, fluff the noodles with chopsticks (or two forks) to separate strands. Cover with sauce and toss well. Garnish with cilantro and serve immediately.

◄ HAZELNUT YAM WONTON WITH MAPLE SYRUP (PAGE 178)

Shanghai Noodles with Shredded Chinese Cabbage, Walnuts and Spicy Bean Paste

Serves 4

Most nuts absorb moisture over time and often taste a little stale. Browning them in a hot oven rejuvenates their real taste.

Preheat oven to 375° F (190° C)
Baking sheet

1 lb	fresh Shanghai noodles *or* 8 oz (250 g) dried spaghetti	500 g
1 tbsp	vegetable oil, plus oil for coating noodles	15 mL
1 cup	whole walnut pieces	250 mL
1 tbsp	maple syrup *or* honey	15 mL
	Salt and pepper	
1	onion, sliced	1
3 cups	shredded Chinese cabbage *or* green cabbage	750 mL
1 tbsp	minced garlic	15 mL
1 tbsp	spicy bean paste	15 mL
2 tbsp	water	25 mL
2 tbsp	sweet soya sauce *or* Sweet Soya Sauce Substitute (see recipe, page 36)	25 mL

1. In a heatproof bowl or pot, cover noodles with boiling water and soak for 5 minutes. (If using pasta, prepare according to package directions.) Coat with a little oil and set aside.

2. Place walnuts on baking sheet and roast for 5 minutes. Drizzle with maple syrup and season with salt and pepper. Return to oven until walnuts have slightly colored, about 5 minutes. Set aside to cool.

3. In a nonstick wok or skillet, heat oil over medium-high heat for 30 seconds. Add onions, cabbage and garlic. Sauté 3 to 4 minutes until cabbage has softened and onions are beginning to color. Add spicy bean paste, water, sweet soya sauce and noodles. Season with salt and pepper and mix well. Cook 1 to 2 minutes until noodles are heated through. Garnish with toasted walnuts and serve immediately.

SIDE DISHES

CHILLED RAMEN WITH SPICY VEGETABLE SAUCE

SERVES 4

Be sure to use Kalamata or any flavorful black olives for this dish — not the bland canned type.

4	packages instant ramen noodles	4
1 tbsp	sesame oil	15 mL

Sauce:

2 tbsp	chili bean sauce	25 mL
2 tbsp	hoisin sauce	25 mL
1 tbsp	oyster sauce *or* soya sauce	15 mL
2 tsp	sugar	10 mL
1/4 cup	vegetable or chicken stock	50 mL
1 tbsp	vegetable oil	15 mL
1/4 cup	chopped onions	50 mL
2 tsp	minced garlic	10 mL
2 tbsp	pitted, chopped Kalamata olives	25 mL
1 cup	chopped mushrooms	250 mL
2 cups	frozen mixed vegetables (carrots, peas and corn)	500 mL
2 tbsp	chopped green onions	25 mL
1	small red chili, seeded and chopped (optional)	1

1. In a large pot of boiling water, cook noodles until just soft, 1 to 2 minutes. Drain, plunge into a bowl of ice water and allow to cool thoroughly. Drain well, toss with sesame oil and set aside.

2. In a small bowl, combine ingredients for sauce.

3. In a nonstick wok or skillet, heat oil over high heat, until just smoking. Add onions, garlic and olives; stir-fry until fragrant, about 1 minute. Add sauce, stir and bring to a boil. Add mushrooms and vegetables; stir. Cover and cook until vegetables are tender, about 3 minutes. Uncover and cook 1 minute until sauce is slightly thickened.

4. Divide noodles into 4 serving bowls. Pour vegetable mixture over noodles. Sprinkle with green onions and chili, if using. Serve immediately.

GAILAN AND OYSTER SAUCE LO MEIN

SERVES 4 TO 6

Gailan (or Chinese broccoli) is wonderful in this dish, but any other kind of Chinese green — or even broccoli or rapini — will do just fine.

If gailan stems are more than 1/2 inch (1 cm) in diameter, cut them in half or quarters before cooking to ensure even and fast cooking.

1 lb	fresh thin egg noodles *or* 8 oz (250 g) dried angel hair pasta	500 mL
2 tsp	sesame oil, plus oil for coating noodles	10 mL
1 tbsp	vegetable oil	15 mL
1 lb	*gailan*, cut into 2-inch (5 cm) lengths *or* broccoli *or* rapini	500 mL
2 tsp	minced garlic	10 mL
1/4 cup	chicken stock	50 mL
1/4 cup	oyster sauce	50 mL
2 tsp	minced ginger root	10 mL
1 tbsp	toasted sesame seeds (optional)	15 mL

1. In a large pot of boiling salted water, cook noodles until *al dente*, about 1 1/2 minutes. (If using pasta, prepare according to package directions.) Drain and toss with a little sesame oil. Transfer to serving dish and keep warm.

2. In a nonstick wok or skillet, heat oil over medium-high heat for 30 seconds. Add *gailan* (or substitute) and stir until well coated, about 30 seconds. Add garlic and stock and stir briefly. Cover and cook until *gailan* is just tender, about 3 minutes. Remove skillet from heat. Remove vegetables with a slotted spoon and arrange over noodles.

3. Add oyster sauce and ginger root to skillet and bring to a boil; cook 30 seconds until heated through. Pour sauce evenly over vegetables and noodles. Sprinkle with sesame seeds, if desired, and serve immediately.

Chinese Noodle and Scallion Rosti

Serves 4

8 oz	dried Chinese-style noodles or dried fettuccine	250 g
1/4 cup	cornstarch	50 mL
2 tbsp	fish sauce	25 mL
4	green onions, cut diagonally into thin strips	4
	Freshly ground black pepper, to taste	
	Vegetable spray	

1. In a large pot of boiling salted water, cook noodles until *al dente*, about 3 minutes. (If using pasta, prepare according to package directions.) Drain and divide noodles into 8 portions.

2. In a bowl, sprinkle one portion of noodles with one eighth of the cornstarch, the fish sauce and the green onion. Toss until well coated. Form mixture into a 6-inch (15 cm) round cake. Repeat with remaining portions of noodles to create 8 cakes.

3. In a nonstick wok or skillet sprayed with vegetable spray, cook noodle cakes, one at a time, over high heat, pressing down on noodles with a spatula to flatten. Turn when bottom is golden, about 1 to 2 minutes per side. When both sides are cooked, season with black pepper. Serve rosti with stir-fried vegetables, meats, or by themselves as a snack.

STEAMED RICE NOODLE CAKES

This easy-to-make recipe can be used as a base for many different toppings — try serving it under a green salad tossed in your favorite dressing.

If you don't have a steamer, pan-fry cakes in a little oil over medium heat until just golden and lightly crisp, about 1 minute per side.

Cakes can be prepared up to 2 hours ahead. Follow recipe to the end of step 3; allow cakes to cool and steam briefly to reheat, or pan-fry until golden and crisp, or reheat in a microwave oven.

Steamer, preferably bamboo

7 oz	thin rice vermicelli (thin rice stick noodles)	200 g
1/4 cup	cornstarch	50 mL
1/2 tsp	salt	2 mL
1/2 tsp	ground pepper	2 mL
2 tbsp	finely chopped cilantro *or* green onions	25 mL
1 tbsp	sesame oil	15 mL
4 tbsp	NUOC CHAM (see recipe, page 33) (optional)	60 mL

1. In a heatproof bowl or pot, cover noodles with boiling water and soak for 3 minutes. Drain. Using chopsticks (or two forks), toss noodles lightly to dry. Divide noodles into 4 equal portions.

2. In a small bowl, combine cornstarch, salt and pepper; mix well. Sprinkle a noodle portion with one quarter of the cornstarch mixture, the cilantro and the green onions. Toss until well distributed. Form noodle mixture into a 6-inch (15 cm) round cake, using a spatula to flatten.

3. Brush steamer rack lightly with sesame oil and place over rapidly boiling water. Place one noodle cake on steamer rack and press down to firm. Cover and steam for 2 minutes. Remove cake and cover with plastic wrap to keep warm. Repeat procedure for remaining cakes.

4. Just before serving, sprinkle each cake with 1 tbsp (15 mL) NUOC CHAM, if desired, and top with entrée of your choice.

CHINESE RATATOUILLE RAMEN NOODLES

SERVES 4

This is a fresh take on that old favorite, spaghetti in tomato sauce.

Try to use Chinese or Japanese eggplants as they're more tender.

If you like more zip, add some chili bean paste.

1 tbsp	vegetable oil	15 mL
1	medium onion, chopped	1
2 tbsp	chopped ginger root	25 mL
1 tbsp	chopped garlic	15 mL
1	Chinese eggplant, diced	1
1	zucchini, diced	1
2	tomatoes, coarsely chopped	2
1/2 cup	chicken stock	125 mL
1/2 tsp	salt	2 mL
1 tbsp	hoisin sauce	15 mL
1 tbsp	soya sauce	15 mL
	Sugar to taste	
	Black pepper to taste	
1-2 tsp	chili bean sauce (optional)	5-10 mL
2 tbsp	chopped green onions	25 mL
3	packages ramen noodles, flavor packets discarded	3
2 tsp	sesame oil	10 mL

1. In a nonstick wok or skillet, heat oil over medium-high heat for 30 seconds. Add onion, ginger root and garlic; sauté for 1 minute. Add eggplant and sauté for 2 minutes. Add tomatoes and stock; bring to boil. Cover and cook for 2 minutes. Add zucchini and stir for 1 minute. Season with salt, hoisin sauce, soya sauce, sugar, pepper and chili bean sauce, if using. Remove from heat. Stir in green onions; keep warm.

2. In a large pot of boiling salted water, cook noodles until just soft, about 1 minute. Drain and toss with sesame oil. Transfer to a serving dish or large platter. Cover with ratatouille.

CILANTRO PARMESAN NOODLES

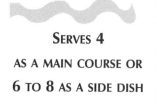

SERVES 4

**AS A MAIN COURSE OR
6 TO 8 AS A SIDE DISH**

*This quick and easy
noodle dish is one of our
standbys. Add some
grilled chicken and a big,
green salad and you can
have a delicious and
nutritious dinner in less
than 20 minutes.*

1 lb	fresh Shanghai noodles *or* fresh fettuccine	500 g
2 tbsp	whipping (35%) cream	25 mL
1/2 cup	freshly grated Parmesan cheese	125 mL
1/2 cup	chopped cilantro	125 mL
	Salt and pepper to taste	

1. In a large pot of boiling salted water, cook noodles until *al dente*, about 3 minutes. (If using pasta, prepare according to package instructions.) Drain.

2. Immediately return noodles to pot. Over low heat, add cream and Parmesan; mix. Add cilantro and toss thoroughly to combine. Season to taste with salt and pepper. Serve immediately.

GINGER AND SCALLION LO MEIN

SERVES 4 TO 6

AS A SIDE DISH

Lo Mein describes a technique that generally involves mixing a flavoring sauce with blanched noodles, requiring no further cooking. This classic Chinese noodle shop dish is often served with a small bowl of broth on the side, in case the noodles are too dry.

1 tbsp	vegetable oil, plus oil for coating noodles	15 mL
1/2 cup	finely chopped green onions	125 mL
2 tbsp	minced ginger root	25 mL
2 tbsp	chicken stock	25 mL
1/2 tsp	salt, or to taste	2 mL
1 lb	fresh wunton noodles or 8 oz (250 g) dried thin egg noodles	500 g

1. In a nonstick wok or skillet, heat oil over medium heat for 30 seconds. Add ginger root and green onions and stir-fry for 30 seconds. Add chicken stock and salt; cook for 1 minute. Remove from heat.

2. In a large pot of boiling salted water, cook noodles until *al dente*, about 2 minutes. (If using dried noodles, prepare according to package directions.) Drain.

3. Immediately transfer noodles to a serving bowl, add sauce and toss to mix. Serve hot as an accompaniment.

CHINESE PESTO

**YIELDS 1 CUP
(250 ML)**

A West Coast/Asian variation of the classic Italian pesto. For a treat, try it on grilled oysters.

2 tsp	minced garlic	10 mL
1 cup	toasted hazelnuts	250 mL
1/2 cup	cilantro leaves, well packed	125 mL
2 tbsp	olive oil	25 mL
	Salt and pepper to taste	

1. In a food processor, combine first 4 ingredients. Process until mixture is a fine paste, scraping down the sides of the bowl once. Season with salt and pepper; pulse until well combined.

PECAN SCALLION SAUCE

**YIELDS 1 CUP
(250 mL)**

This delicious sauce adds instant flavor to cooked noodles or pasta, or grilled meats and fish.

1/4 cup	olive oil	50 mL
2 tbsp	minced ginger root	25 mL
1/2 cup	chopped green onions	125 mL
1/2 cup	toasted pecans	125 mL
1/4 cup	chicken stock	50 mL
	Salt and pepper to taste	

1. In a food processor, combine all ingredients except chicken stock and salt and pepper. Pulse to a paste, thinning with stock, until mixture has consistency of a thick sauce. Season with salt and pepper to taste. Transfer to a small pot and, over low heat, warm until just warmed through, about 2 minutes. Set aside to allow flavors to blend.

*D*ESSERTS

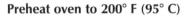

PAN-FRIED BLUEBERRY AND CREAM CHEESE GYOZA WITH A LEMON-GINGER SAUCE

SERVES 6 TO 8

Gyoza are Japanese dumplings that are usually stuffed with meat or vegetables. Here we've turned that technique into a fast and elegant dessert.

The small, round dumpling wrappers are usually found in the freezer section of Asian markets.

Preheat oven to 200° F (95° C)

Sauce:

1 cup	water	250 mL
4 tbsp	sugar	60 mL
1 tbsp	liquid honey	15 mL
1 tsp	grated ginger root	5 mL
	Juice and zest of 1 lemon	

Dumplings:

1 cup	fresh or frozen blueberries	250 mL
1/2 cup	cream cheese, softened	125 mL
3 tbsp	sugar	45 mL
24	round wonton wrappers	24
1	egg beaten with 1 tsp (5 mL) water	1
1 tbsp	vegetable oil	15 mL

1. In a small saucepan over medium heat, combine water, sugar, honey, ginger root, lemon juice and zest. Once the sugar is dissolved, reduce heat to low and simmer until mixture is reduced to a thick syrup, about 15 minutes. Remove from heat and set aside.

2. In a small bowl, gently combine blueberries, cream cheese and sugar.

3. On a work surface, lay out 6 wonton wrappers. Using a pastry brush, coat each round with egg mixture. Place 1 heaping teaspoon (5-7 mL) of blueberry filling in the center of each wonton and fold to form a half moon. Press edges to seal. Repeat until all the filling is used.

4. In a nonstick skillet, heat oil over medium heat for 30 seconds. Cook dumplings, 6 at a time, until golden, 2 to 3 minutes per side. Transfer to a plate and keep warm in oven. Repeat with remaining dumplings. To serve, drizzle ginger-lemon sauce over dumplings.

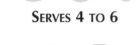

THIN EGG NOODLE AND BLACK PLUM CLAFOUTI

SERVES 4 TO 6

Clafouti, a specialty of southern France, is often made with seasonal fruit such as cherries. Our version adds the texture of thin eggs noodles.

Almost any fruit can be substituted for the plums.

Preheat oven to 350° F (180° C)
10-inch square (3 L) casserole dish, buttered

4 oz	thin dried egg noodles	125 g
	Vegetable oil for coating noodles	
4	eggs	4
2 cups	milk	500 mL
1/2 cup	flour	125 mL
1/2 cup	sugar	125 mL
2 tsp	ground cinnamon	10 mL
10	black plums	10
	Icing sugar, to taste	

1. In a large pot of boiling salted water, cook the noodles until *al dente*, about 3 to 4 minutes. Drain, toss with a little oil and set aside.

2. In a medium-sized mixing bowl, beat eggs until frothy. Add milk and mix well. Add flour, sugar and cinnamon; blend until smooth. Add noodles and toss to coat.

3. On a cutting board, cut plums in half. Remove pit and arrange halves in bottom of prepared dish. Top with batter and bake for 1 hour or until a toothpick inserted in the center emerges clean. Let the clafouti cool in pan until lukewarm. Serve warm with a dusting of icing sugar.

RIESLING AND HONEY POACHED PEARS ON A CINNAMON-SUGAR CRISPY NOODLE PANCAKE

SERVES 4

Crispy noodles and soft poached fruit is a delightful combination.

The poaching broth can be reduced to a syrup and used to glaze the fruit.

The recipe can be prepared to the end of step 3 up to 1 day in advance.

Parchment paper

Pears:

4	firm Anjou or Bartlett pears *or* any tart cooking apple	4
1/2 tsp	lemon juice	2 mL
1/2 cup	white sugar	125 mL
2 tbsp	honey	25 mL
2 cups	water	500 mL
1/2 cup	Riesling or any fruity white wine	125 mL

Pancakes:

4 oz	fresh chow mein noodles	125 g
1 tbsp	vegetable oil, plus oil for coating noodles	15 mL
4 tbsp	white sugar	60 mL
1 tsp	ground cinnamon	5 mL

1. On a cutting board, peel pears and cut in half, scooping out seeds and core with a small spoon. In a bowl large enough to accommodate the pears, combine lemon juice and enough water to cover the pears. Set aside.

2. In a large, heavy-bottomed saucepan over medium heat, cook sugar and honey until the sugar begins to caramelize into a deep mahogany color. Carefully add the water to the pan (the mixture will sputter violently). Add wine. Bring to a boil and cook until the caramel is totally dissolved. Add pears, cover with parchment paper and simmer for 30 minutes or until the pears are soft but still firm. Remove from heat and let cool in the caramel mixture.

3. In a heatproof bowl or pot, cover noodles with boiling water and soak for 3 minutes. Drain and toss with a little vegetable oil.

4. In a small bowl, mix the sugar and cinnamon together. Set aside.

5. In a nonstick skillet, heat oil over medium heat for 30 seconds. Add noodles in 4 small rounds and fry until golden brown, about 5 minutes. Flip, press noodles down with a spatula and cook until golden. Remove from heat and sprinkle each pancake with the cinnamon-sugar mixture. Top with a poached pear and serve while warm.

HAZELNUT YAM WONTON WITH MAPLE SYRUP

SERVES 6 TO 8

The crispy, warm wontons contrast with the smooth, cool ice cream, making this a luscious dessert. If you're not having yams with your holiday dinner, this would add a new twist to a traditional Christmas or Thanksgiving feast.

Preheat oven to 200 °F (95° C)

2 tbsp	butter	25 mL
1 tbsp	brown sugar	15 mL
1 tsp	cinnamon	5 mL
Pinch	nutmeg	Pinch
1	yam, roasted, skinned and mashed	1
1/2 cup	coarsely chopped roasted hazelnuts	125 mL
24	square wonton wrappers	24
1 cup	vegetable oil for frying	250 mL
2 tbsp	maple syrup	25 mL
2 tsp	icing sugar for garnish	10 mL
2 cups	vanilla ice cream, divided into 6 portions	500 mL

1. In a small skillet or saucepan, melt butter over low heat. Remove from heat, add sugar and spices; mix well.

2. In a mixing bowl, combine yam and nuts. Add half butter mixture and mix well.

3. On a work surface, lay out 1 wonton wrapper. Place 1 tbsp (15 mL) filling in center. Brush the edges with remaining butter mixture. Cover with another wonton wrapper, squeeze the air out by pressing with your fingertips and press edges together to seal. Repeat with remaining ingredients until all the filling is used. (You should be able to make 12 wontons.)

4. In a small pot, heat oil until a small piece of wonton wrapper sizzles and immediately floats to the top. Fry wontons one or two at a time until golden, about 20 seconds per side. Place finished wontons on paper towels to drain any excess oil. Keep warm in oven.

5. To serve, place 2 or 3 wontons on each plate, drizzle with maple syrup and dust with icing sugar. Serve vanilla ice cream as an accompaniment.

RICE NOODLE ROLLS STUFFED WITH A HONEY AND MIXED-NUT PASTE

SERVES 6 TO 8

This low-fat dish was inspired by Chinese rice desserts, which are normally filled with sweet red bean or peanut fillings. For a luxurious touch, add a scoop of ice cream or fruit sorbet.

Preheat oven to 375° F (190° C)

Baking sheet and parchment paper

1 cup	hazelnuts	250 mL
1 cup	pecans	250 mL
1 cup	shredded, unsweetened coconut	250 mL
2 tbsp	honey	25 mL
4	fresh rice noodle rolls	4
1 tbsp	melted butter	15 mL

1. On a baking sheet, roast hazelnuts until toasted and beginning to brown, about 5 to 8 minutes. Remove, place in a clean kitchen towel and rub contents briskly to remove skin. Pick out nuts and discard the skins.

2. On same baking sheet, roast pecans and coconut until the coconut begins to color, about 5 or 6 minutes.

3. Add hazelnuts, pecans and coconut to the bowl of food processor. Process until mixture resembles a coarse meal. Transfer to a small bowl. Add honey and mix to form a paste.

4. Unroll a rice noodle sheet on a work surface. Place one eighth of the nut mixture in a smooth layer along the top of the sheet, then roll up to form a compact log. Repeat with remaining sheets and filling.

5. Cut each log into 4 pieces. Place on baking sheet lined with parchment paper and brush with melted butter. The rolls can be made in advance to this point.

6. Just before serving, bake the rolls for 5 to 8 minutes until warmed through. Remove from oven and serve immediately.

INDEX